THE
MYSTIQUE OF
ENLIGHTENMENT

My teaching, if that is the word you want to use, has no copyright. You are free to reproduce, distribute, interpret, misinterpret, distort, garble, do what you like, even claim authorship, without my consent or the permission of anybody.

The Mystique of Enlightenment

The Radical Ideas of U. G. Krishnamurti

Edited by
Rodney Arms

SENTIENT PUBLICATIONS, LLC

First Sentient Publications edition, 2002

Printed in the United States of America

Cover Design by Ray Lundgren

Book Design by Ana Dayva

Publisher's Cataloging-in-Publication Data

Krishnamurti, U. G. (Uppaluri Gopala).
 The mystique of enlightenment : the radical ideas of U. G.
Krishnamurti / U. G. Krishnamurti ; edited by Rodney Arms
  p.   cm.
  ISBN 0-9710786-1-0 (pbk.) Revised ed.
  Originally published: Goa, India: Dinesh Vaghela Cemetile
Corp., 1982.
  1. Spirituality. 2. Spiritual life. 3. Mysticism. 4. Mind and
body. 5. Philosophy of mind. I. Arms, Rodney. II. Title.
291.4—dc21
Library of Congress Control Number: 2001093072

SENTIENT PUBLICATIONS

A Limited Liability Company
1113 Spruce St.
Boulder, CO 80302

www.sentientpublications.com

Contents

Foreword

U. G. Krishnamurti was born in India in 1918 to Brahmin parents and was given a rigorous education in classical Hindu literature. He was raised to take on the mantle of guru, in a manner similar to J. Krishnamurti (to whom U. G. is not related), as his family believed that he had approached enlightenment in a past life. He spent his youth studying with various spiritual teachers, practicing techniques such as yoga and meditation, and examining with a critical mind the practices and teachings he encountered.

As a young man, U. G. attended the University of Madras and studied widely in psychology, science, and philosophy. All his life he had heard about the state of enlightenment, and he was determined to discover by any means possible what it really *was*. He became a popular lecturer for the Theosophical Society, an organization that introduced Eastern spiritual wisdom to the West, founded in 1875 by Madame Blavatsky. U.G.'s grandfather had strong ties to the group, and its founders and members had been frequent visitors to their home during U.G.'s youth.

At age 25, U. G. married and eventually fathered four children.

In the late 1940's, he met J. Krishnamurti, who had been adopted at the age of 14 by the president of the Theosophical Society, Annie Besant. She was convinced that it was J. Krishnamurti's destiny to become a World Teacher, so she directed his education accordingly and formed an organization to support this mission. By the time the two Krishnamurtis were introduced, each had rejected the role of guru for which he had been groomed. For seven years they met daily, struggling to uncover the nature of truth, and parted without resolving their differences in this matter.

U. G. continued lecturing throughout the world. Then in 1961 he began to feel that he was no longer in control of his life. He left his family and went to London without means or purpose. As he describes it, "I was a bum practically, living on the charity of some people and not knowing anything. There was no will. I didn't know what I was doing. I was practically insane." This seemingly aimless period of his life lasted for six years, marked by an intense interest in the question, "What is that state?" He was still trying desperately to understand the state described by all the great spiritual teachers, by Shankara, Buddha, and Jesus. Eventually he came to believe that he was in that state.

Finally, at age 49 on a park bench in Saanen, Switzerland, U. G. experienced what he calls his "calamity." The question "How do I know that I am in that state?" had been occupying him for some time. As he sat and meditated on the question, he realized that there was no answer for it. The question disappeared completely. U. G. then began a physical transformation that lasted seven days, which he says affected every cell in his body. He describes how his senses became extremely acute, and he lost the illusion of the continuity of thought and the sense of a center. "Then thought cannot link up...Every time a thought arises, it explodes. So this continuity comes to an end, and thought falls into its natural rhythm."

U. G. calls this the natural state of man. He does not equate it with enlightenment, which he describes as an illusion created by our culture. He states emphatically that one can do nothing to attain the natural state. In fact, any movement *towards* it separates one *from* it.

In a world in which spiritual techniques, teachers, concepts, and organizations are legion, U. G. stands nearly alone in his rejection of it all. "I am only interested in describing this state, in clearing away the occultation and mystification in which those people in the 'holy business' have shrouded the whole thing. Maybe I can convince you not to waste a lot of time and energy looking for a state that does not exist except in your imagination...The natural state is acausal: it just happens." Since his "calamity," he has spent his time traveling throughout the world, staying with friends or in rented apartments for a few months at a time. He gives no public talks, but meets with people who come to see him. His message is simple: he has no message. Nevertheless, his words can inspire you to face your own assumptions and motivations squarely, and to come to the question that is uniquely yours.

—Publisher

Chapter I

U. G.

Compiled from conversations in India and Switzerland,
1973 to 1976

People call me an enlightened man. I detest that term. They can't find any other word to describe the way I am functioning. At the same time, I point out that there is no such thing as enlightenment at all. I say that because all my life I've searched and wanted to be an enlightened man, and I discovered that there is no such thing as enlightenment at all, and so the question whether a particular person is enlightened or not doesn't arise. I don't give a hoot for a sixth-century-BC Buddha, let alone all the other claimants we have in our midst. They are a bunch of exploiters, thriving on the gullibility of the people. There is no power outside of man. Man has created God out of fear. So the problem is fear and not God.

I discovered for myself and by myself that there is no self to realize. That's the realization I am talking about. It comes as a shattering blow. It hits you like a thunderbolt. You have invested everything in one basket, self-realization, and, in the end, suddenly you discover that there is no self to discover, no self to realize. And you say to yourself, "What the hell have I been doing all my life?!" That blasts you.

All kinds of things happened to me. The physical pain was unbearable. That is why I say you really don't want this. I wish I could give you a glimpse of it, a touch of it. Then you wouldn't want to touch this at all. What you are pursuing doesn't exist; it is a myth. You wouldn't want anything to do with this.

UG: I don't like to use the words *enlightenment, freedom, moksha,* or *liberation.* All these words are loaded words. They have a connotation of their own. This cannot be brought about through any effort of yours. It just happens. And why it happens to one individual and not another, I don't know.

Questioner: *So, it happened to you?*

It happened to me.

When, Sir?

In my forty-ninth year. But whatever you do in the direction of whatever you are after—the pursuit or search for truth or reality—takes you away from your own very natural state, in which you always are. It's not something you can acquire, attain, or accomplish as a result of your effort. That is why I use the word *acausal.* It has no cause, but somehow the search comes to an end.

You think, Sir, that it is not the result of the search? I ask because I have heard that you studied philosophy, that you were associated with religious people.

You see, the search takes you away from yourself. It is in the opposite direction; it has absolutely no relation.

In spite of it, it has happened, not because of it?

In spite of it—yes, that's the word. All that you do makes it impossible for what already is there to express itself. That is why I call this "your natural state." You're always in that state. What prevents what is there from expressing itself in its own way is the search. The search is always in the wrong direction, so all that you consider very profound, all that you consider sacred, is a contamination in that consciousness. You may not like the word *contamination,* but all that you consider sacred, holy, and profound is a contamination.

So, there's nothing that you can do. It's not in your hands. I don't like to use the word *grace,* because if you use the word *grace,* the grace of

whom? You are not a specially chosen individual; you deserve this, I
don't know why.

If it were possible for me, I would be able to help somebody. This is
something that I can't give, because you have it. Why should I give it
to you? It is ridiculous to ask for a thing that you already have.

But I don't feel it, and you do.

No, it is not a question of feeling it; it is not a question of knowing it.
You will never know. You have no way of knowing that at all for yourself; it begins to express itself. You see, I don't know how to put it.
Never does the thought that I am different from anybody come into
my consciousness.

Has it been so from the beginning, ever since you became conscious of yourself?

No, I can't say that. I was after something, like anybody else brought
up in the religious atmosphere—searching for something, pursuing
something. So, to answer that question is not easy, because I'll have to
go into the whole background. Maybe it comes, I don't know. [laughs]

*Just out of curiosity, like Nachiketa, I am very interested in knowing how
these things have happened to you personally, to the extent you are aware of.*

You see, that's a long story; it's not so simple.

We would like to hear it.

No, you see, I will have to tell you about my whole life. It will take me
a long time. My life story goes up to a point, and then it stops. There
is no more biography after that.

The two biographers who are interested in writing my biography
have two different approaches. One says that what I did—the sadhana
[spiritual exercises], education, the whole background—put me there.
I say it was in spite of all that. [laughter] The other biographer isn't
much interested in my statement "in spite of," because there isn't much
material for him to write a big volume. [laughter] They are more interested in that. The publishers too are interested in that kind of thing.

That is very natural because you are operating in a field where the cause and effect relationship always operates. That is why you are interested in finding out the cause, how this kind of a thing happened. So, we are back where we started, square number one. We are still concerned with "how."

My background is worthless. It can't be a model for anybody, because your background is unique. Every event in your life is something unique in its own way. Your conditions, your environment, your background—the whole thing is different. Every event in your life is different.

I don't seek a model to give to the rest of the world. I'm not asking from that angle. We see a star, we see the sun, we see the moon. It is like that; not that I would like to imitate you. It may be relevant, who knows? That is why I said I am Nachiketa here. I don't want to leave without knowing the truth from you.

You need a Yama Dharmaraja to answer your questions.

If you don't mind, you be Yama Dharmaraja.

I don't mind. Help me. You see, I'm helpless. I don't know where to begin. Where to end, I know. [laughter] I think I will have to tell the whole story of my life.

We don't mind listening.

It doesn't come.

You need to be inspired.

I am not inspired, and I am the last person to inspire anybody. I will have to tell you, to satisfy your curiosity, the other side, the shoddy side of my life.

[He was born July 9, 1918 in South India into an upper-middle-class Brahmin family. The family name being Uppaluri, he was given the name Uppaluri Gopala Krishnamurti. His mother died soon after his birth, and he was brought up by his maternal grandparents in the small town of Gudivada near Masulipatam.]

I was brought up in a very religious atmosphere. My grandfather was a very cultured man. He knew Blavatsky [the founder of the Theosophical Society] and Olcott, and then, later on, the second and third generation of Theosophists. They all visited our house. He was a great lawyer, a very rich man, a very cultured man and, very strangely, a very orthodox man. He was a sort of mixed-up kid: orthodoxy, tradition on one side, and then the opposite, Theosophy and the whole thing, on the other side. He failed to establish a balance. That was the beginning of my problem.

[UG was often told that his mother had said, just before she died, that he "was born to a destiny immeasurably high." His grandfather took this very seriously and gave up his law practice to devote himself to UG's upbringing and education. His grandparents and their friends were convinced that he was a yoga bhrashta, one who had come within inches of enlightenment in his past life.]

My father had learned men on his payroll, and he dedicated himself, for some reason—I don't want to go into the whole business—to create a profound atmosphere for me and to educate me in the right way, inspired by the Theosophists and the whole lot. And so, every morning those fellows would come and read the Upanishads, Panchadasi, Naishkarmya Siddhi, the commentaries, the commentaries on commentaries, the whole lot, from four o'clock to six o'clock, and this little boy of five, six, or seven years had to listen to all that crap. So much so that by the time I reached my seventh year I could repeat most of those things, the passages from the Panchadasi, Naishkarmya Siddhi and this, that, and the other. So many holy men visited my house—the Ramakrishna Order and the others. You name it, and those fellows had somehow visited that house. That was an open house for every holy man. So, one thing I discovered when I was quite young was that they were all hypocrites. They said something, they believed something, and their lives were shallow, nothing. That was the beginning of my search.

My grandfather used to meditate. (He is dead, and I don't want to say anything bad about him.) He used to meditate for one or two hours in a separate meditation room. One day a little baby, one and a half or two years old, started crying for some reason. That chap came down and started beating the child, and the child almost turned blue—and this man, you see, meditating two hours every day. I thought, "Look! What is this he has done?" That posed a sort of (I don't want to use the psychological term, but there is no escape from it) a traumatic experience. I thought, "There must be something funny about the whole business of meditation. Their lives are shallow, empty. They talk marvelously, express things in a very beautiful way, but what about their lives? There is this neurotic fear in their lives. They say something, but it doesn't operate in their lives. What is wrong with them?" Not that I sat in judgment over those people.

Things went on and on and on, so I got involved with these things. "Is there anything to what they profess—the Buddha, Jesus, the great teachers? Everybody is talking about moksha, liberation, freedom. What is that? I want to know for myself. These are all useless fellows, yet there must be some person in this world who is an embodiment and apostle of all those things. If there is one, I want to find out for myself."

Then so many things happened. There was one man called Sivananda Saraswati in those days. He was the evangelist of Hinduism. Between the ages of fourteen and twenty-one (I am skipping many of the unnecessary events) I used to go there and meet him very often, and I did everything, all the austerities. I was so young, but I was determined to find out if there was any such thing as moksha, and I wanted that moksha for myself. I wanted to prove to myself and to everybody that there cannot be any hypocrisy in such people, so I practiced yoga, I practiced meditation, studied everything. I experienced every kind of experience that the books talked about—samadhi, supersamadhi, nirvikalpa samadhi, everything. Then I said to myself, "Thought can create any experience you want—bliss, beatitude, ecstasy, melting away into nothingness—all those experiences. So, this can't be the thing, because I'm the same person, mechanically doing these things. Meditations have no value for me. This is not leading me anywhere."

Then, you see, sex became a tremendous problem for me, a young human boy. "This is something natural, a biological thing, an urge in the human body. Why do these people all want to deny this sex and suppress something very natural, something that is part of the whole thing, in order to get something else? This is more real, more important to me than moksha and liberation and all that. This is a reality. I think of gods and goddesses and I have wet dreams. Why should I feel guilty? It's something natural; I have no control over this kind of thing happening. Meditation has not helped me, study has not helped me, my disciplines have not helped me. I never touch salt; I never touch chilies or any spices." Then one day I found this man Sivananada eating mango pickles behind closed doors. "Here is a man who has denied himself everything in the hope of getting something, but that fellow cannot control himself. He is a hypocrite." I don't want to say anything bad about him. "This kind of life is not for me."

Between your fourteenth and twenty-first year, you say, you felt a great urge for sex. Did you marry then?

No, I didn't rush; I allowed that. I wanted to experience the sex urge. "Suppose you don't do anything, what happens to that?" I wanted to understand this whole business. "Why do I want to indulge in these auto-eroticisms? I don't know anything about sex. Then why is it that I have all kinds of images of sex?" This was my inquiry; this was my meditation—not sitting in lotus posture or standing on my head. "How am I able to form these images?" I never went to a movie; I never looked at, you know, now you have all kinds of posters. "How is it? This is something inside, not put in from outside. The outside is stimulating; stimulation comes from outside. But there is another kind of stimulation from inside. This is more important to me. I can cut out all that external stimulation successfully, but how can I cut out this from inside?" I wanted to find this out.

And then, I was also interested in finding out what this sex experience was. Although I myself had not experienced sex, I seemed to know what that sex experience was like. This went on and on and on. I did not rush to have sex with a woman or anything; I allowed things to happen in their own way. That was a time when I didn't want to marry. My aim was to become an ascetic, a monk, and all that kind of thing— not marriage. But things happened and I said to myself, "If it is a question of satisfying your sex urge, why not marry? That is what society is there for. Why should you go and have sex with some woman? You can have a natural expression of sex in marriage."

I arrived at a point when I was twenty-one where I felt very strongly that all teachers—Buddha, Jesus, Sri Ramakrishna, everybody—kidded themselves, deluded themselves, and deluded everybody. This, you see, could not be the thing at all. "Where is the state that these people talk about and describe? That description seems to have no relation to me, to the way I am functioning. Everybody says, 'Don't get angry.' I am angry all the time. I'm full of brutal activities inside, so that is false. What these people are telling me I should be is something false, and because it is false it will falsify me. I don't want to live the life of a false person. I am greedy, and non-greed is what they are talking about. There is something wrong somewhere. This greed is something real, something natural to me; what they are talking about is unnatural. So, something is wrong somewhere. But I am not ready to change myself, to falsify myself, for the sake of being in a state of non-greed. My greed is a reality to me." I lived in the midst of people who talked of these things everlastingly. Everybody was false, I can tell you. So, somehow, what you call existentialist nausea (I didn't use those words at the time, but now I happen to know these terms), revulsion against everything sacred and everything holy, crept into my system and threw everything out. "No more slokas, no more religion, no more practices. There isn't anything there; but what is here is something natural. I am a brute; I am a monster; I am full of violence. This is reality. I am full of desire. Desirelessness, non-greed, non-anger—those things have no meaning to me. They are false, and they are not only false, they are falsifying me." So I said to myself, "I'm finished with the whole business." But it is not that simple, you see.

Then somebody came along, and we were discussing all these things. He found me practically an atheist (but not a practicing atheist), skeptical of everything, heretical down to my boots. He said "There is one man here, somewhere in Madras at Tiruvannamalai, called Ramana Maharshi. Come on, let's go and see that man. Here is a living human embodiment of the Hindu tradition."

I didn't want to see any holy man. If you have seen one, you have seen them all. I never shopped around, went around searching for people, sitting at the feet of the masters, learning something, because everybody tells you, "Do more and more of the same thing, and you will get it." What I got were more and more experiences, and then those experiences demanded permanence, and there is no such thing as permanence. So, "The holy men are all phonies. They are telling me only what is there in the books. That I can read. 'Do the same again and again.' That I don't want. Experiences I don't want. They are trying to share an experience with me. I'm not interested in experience. As far as experience goes, for me there is no difference between the religious experience and the sex experience or any other experience. The religious experience is like any other experience. I am not interested in experiencing Brahman; I am not interested in experiencing reality; I am not interested in experiencing truth. They might help others, but they cannot help me. I'm not interested in doing more of the same. What I have done is enough. At school if you want to solve a mathematical problem, you repeat it again and again. You solve the mathematical problem, and you discover that the answer is in the problem. So, what the hell are you doing, trying to solve the problem? It is easier to find the answer first instead of going through all this."

So, reluctantly, hesitatingly, unwilling, I went to see Ramana Maharshi. That fellow dragged me. He said, "Go there once. Something will happen to you." He talked about it and gave me a book, *Search in Secret India* by Paul Brunton, so I read the chapter relating to this man.

"All right, I don't mind, let me go and see." That man was sitting there. From his very presence I felt, "What! This man—how can he help me? This fellow who is reading comic strips, cutting vegetables, playing with this, that, or the other—how can this man help me? He can't help me." Anyway, I sat there. Nothing happened. I looked at him, and he looked at me. "In his presence you feel silent, your questions disappear, his look changes you." All that remained a story, fancy stuff to me. I sat there. There were a lot of questions inside, silly questions. So, "The questions have not disappeared. I have been sitting here for two hours, and the questions are still there. All right, let me ask him some questions." Because at that time I very much wanted moksha. This part of my background, moksha, I wanted. "You are supposed to be a liberated man." I didn't say that. "Can you give me what you have?" I asked him this question, but that man didn't answer, so after some lapse of time I repeated that question. "I am asking, 'Whatever you have, can you give it to me?'"

He said, "I can give you, but can you take it?" Boy! For the first time this fellow says that he has something and that I can't take it. Nobody before had said "I can give you," but this man said, "I can give you, but can you take it?" Then I said to myself, "If there is any individual in this world who can take it, it is me, because I have done so much sadhana, seven years of sadhana. He can think that I can't take it, but I can take it. If I can't take it, who can take it?" That was my frame of mind at the time. You know, I was so confident of myself.

I didn't stay with him, I didn't read any of his books. I asked him a few more questions. "Can one be free sometimes and not free sometimes?"

He said, "Either you are free, or you are not free at all." There was another question that I don't remember. He answered in a very strange way. "There are no steps leading you to that." But I ignored all these things. These questions didn't matter to me. The answers didn't interest me at all.

But this question, "Can you take it?" "How arrogant he is!" That was my feeling. "Why can't I take it, whatever it is? What is it that he has?" That was my question, a natural question. So, the question formulated itself. "What is that state that all those people—Buddha, Jesus and the whole gang—were in? Ramana is in that state—supposed to be, I don't know. But that chap is like me, a human being. How is he different from me? What others say or what he is saying is of no importance to me. Anybody can do what he is doing. What is there? He can't be very much different from me. He was also born from parents. He has his own particular ideas about the whole business. Some people say something happened to him, but how is he different from me? What is there? What is that state?" That was my fundamental question, the basic question. That went on and on and on. "I must find out what that state is. Nobody can give that state. I am on my own. I have to go on this uncharted sea without a compass, without a boat, with not even a raft to take me. I am going to find out for myself what the state is in which that man is." I wanted that very much, otherwise I wouldn't have given my life.

This giving-taking business, I don't understand.

I can't say anything about what he meant when he said, "I can give it, but can you take it?" But in a way that helped me to formulate my own question. You see, if somebody were to ask me a similar question now, I would say there isn't anything to get from anybody. Who am I to give it to you? You have what I have. We are all at 25 Sannidhi Street, and you are asking me, "Where is 25 Sannidhi Street?" I say you are there.

Not that I know I am there. This wanting to know where you are—you are asking that question.

[UG says he never again visited Ramana or any of "those religious people," and never again touched any religious book except to study for his philosophy examinations.]

Then my real search began. All my religious background was there in me. Then I started exploring. For some years I studied psychology and also philosophy (Eastern and Western), mysticism, all the modern sciences—everything, the whole area of human knowledge. I started exploring on my own. The search went on and on and on, and "What is that state?" was my question, and the question had an intensity of its own. So, "All this knowledge doesn't satisfy me. Why read all this?" Psychology was one of my subjects for a Master's degree. Unfortunately, at that time it was part of our syllabus. I was interested in psychology for the simple reason that the mind had always intrigued me. "Where is this mind? I want to know something about it. Here, inside of me, I don't see any mind, but all these books talk of mind. Come on, let me see what the Western psychologists have to say about the mind." One day I asked my professor, "We are talking about the mind all the time. Do you know for yourself what the mind is? We are studying so many books—Freud, Jung, Adler and the whole gang. All that stuff I know. I read the definitions and descriptions that are there in the books. But do you yourself know anything about the mind?"

He said, "Don't ask such inconvenient questions. [laughter] They are very dangerous questions. If you want to pass the examination, just take down these notes, memorize them, and repeat them in the answer papers. You will get your degree."

"I am not interested in a degree; I am interested in finding out about the mind."

[His grandfather died, and UG left the University of Madras without completing his degree. In 1943 he married.]

Then I got involved with the Theosophical Society, because of my background. I inherited the Theosophical Society, J. Krishnamurti, and a lot of money from my grandfather. So that made it easy for me. Plenty of money was there at that time—fifty or sixty thousand dollars—so I could do all this kind of thing. I got involved with the Theosophical Society as a lecturer [and eventually UG was elected Joint General Secretary of the Society in India], but my heart was not in it. "All this is second-hand information. What is the point of giving lectures?" I was a very good speaker at that time, but not any more. I was a first-class speaker, lecturing everywhere, on every platform. I addressed every university in India. "This is not something real to me. Anybody who has brains can gather this information and then throw it out. What am I doing? Why am I wasting my time? This is not my living, not my means of livelihood. If it is your living, all right, then I can understand. You repeat like a parrot and make a living, but this is not my living. And yet, I am interested in something. I am interested in that kind of thing."

Then [in the late 1940's, towards the end of UG's time with the Theosophical Society] J. Krishnamurti arrived on the scene. He had just returned from the United States.

Are you related to J. Krishnamurti?

"Krishnamurti" is only a given name, not a family name. His family name is Jiddu. Krishnamurti is quite a common name—Jiddu Krishnamurti.

I got involved with him. I listened to him for some seven years, every time he came. I didn't meet him personally, because the whole "World Teacher" business and all that created some kind of a distance. "How can a World Teacher be created? World Teachers are born, not made." That was my kind of make-up. I knew the whole background, the whole business. I was not part of the inner circle. I was always on the periphery; I never wanted to involve myself. There was the same hypocrisy there too, in the sense that there was nothing in their lives. They were shallow—the scholars, masterminds, and remarkable people. "What is this? What is there behind?"

Then Krishnamurti came along, and after seven years circumstances brought us together. I met him every day. We discussed the whole thing. I was not interested in his abstractions at all. His teaching did not interest me at all. I told him once, "You have picked up the psychological jargon of the day, and you are trying to express something through this jargon. You adopt analysis and arrive at the point that analysis is not it. This kind of analysis is only paralyzing people; it is not helping people. It is paralyzing me." My question was the same question: "What is it that you have? The abstractions that you are throwing at me, I am not interested in. Is there anything behind the abstractions? What is that? Somehow I have a feeling—I can't say why—that what is behind the abstractions you are throwing out is what I am interested in. For some reason I have a feeling—it may be my own projection. You (to give a familiar, traditional simile) may not have tasted the sugar, but at least you seem to have looked at the sugar. The way you are describing things gives me the feeling that you have at least seen the sugar, but I am not certain that you have tasted the sugar."

So, we struggled for years and years. [laughs] There were some personal differences between us. I wanted some straight, honest answers from him, which he did not give, for his own reasons. He was very defensive. "What is there for you to defend? Hang your past, the whole thing, on a tree and leave it to the people. Why do you want to defend yourself?" I wanted some straight, honest answers about his background, which he didn't give me in a satisfactory way. And then, towards the end, I insisted, "Come on, is there anything behind the abstractions which you are throwing at me?"

And that chappie said, "You have no way of knowing it for yourself." Finish. That was the end of our relationship, you see.

"If I have no way of knowing it, you have no way of communicating it. What the hell are we doing? I've wasted seven years. Goodbye, I don't want to see you again." Then I walked out.

[It was probably about this time that UG was puzzled by the appearance of certain psychic powers.]

Before my forty-ninth year I had so many powers, so many experiences, but I didn't pay any attention to them. The moment I saw a man, I could see the entire past, present, and future of that man without his telling me anything. I didn't use them. I was wondering, puzzled, you see. "Why do I have this power?" Sometimes I said things, and they always happened. I couldn't figure out the mechanism of that. I tried to. "How is it possible for me to say something like that?" They always happened. Then it had certain unpleasant consequences and created suffering for some people.

[UG was traveling all over the world, still lecturing. In 1955 he and his wife and four children moved to the United States in search of treatment for his eldest son's polio. By 1961 his money was finished, and he felt beginning within him a tremendous upheaval which he could not and did not wish to control, and which was to last six years and end with the "calamity" (as he calls his entry into the natural state). His marriage broke up. He put his family on a plane to India, and he went to London. He arrived penniless and began roaming the city. For three years he lived idly in the streets. His friends saw him heading on a headlong course downhill, but he says that at the time his life seemed perfectly natural to him. Later, religious-minded people were to use the mystic's phrase "the dark night of the soul" to describe those years, but in his view there was "no heroic struggle with temptation and worldliness, no soul-wrestling with urges, no poetic climaxes, but just a simple withering away of the will."]

It was as if there was no head for me after that: "Where is my head? Do I have a head or not? The head seems to be there. Where do these thoughts come from?" This was my question. The head was absent, and only the body was moving around. There was no will to do anything. It was like a leaf blown here, there, and everywhere, living a shoddy life. It went on and on and on. Finally—I don't know what happened—one day I said to myself, "This kind of life is no good." I was a bum practically, living on the charity of some people and not knowing anything. There was no will. I didn't know what I was doing. I was practically insane. I was in London, wandering in the streets—no place to live—wandering in the streets all night. The policemen always stopped me. "Don't you have a place? We will put you in the nick." So, that was the kind of life I led. Daytimes I would go and sit in the British Museum—I could get a ticket. What to read in the British Museum? I was not interested in reading at all; no books interested me. But to pretend that I was there to read something, I used to pick up a thesaurus of underground slang—the underground men, the criminals—all kinds of slang. I was reading that for some time to spend the day. At night I'd go somewhere. It went on and on and on.

One day I was sitting in Hyde Park. The policeman came and said, "You can't stay here. We are going to throw you out." Where to go? What to do? No money—I think I only had five pence in my pocket. The thought came into my head: "Go to the Ramakrishna Mission." That's all, just that thought out of nowhere—maybe it was all my own projection.

There was no way for me except wandering in the streets, and that fellow was after me, so I took the tube up to a point until I couldn't go any further. From there I walked to the Mission to meet the Swami. They said, "You can't see him now. It is ten o'clock in the night. He won't see you; he won't see anybody at all." I told the secretary I had to see him. Somehow he came.

Then I put this scrapbook before him. This was me—my lectures, The New York Times' comments on my lectures, my background. Somehow I had kept that book with me, the scrapbook that my manager had prepared in America. "This was me, and is me now."

Then he said, "What do you want?"

I said, "I want to go into the meditation room and sit there all night."

He said, "That you can't do. We have a policy not to let anybody use the meditation room after eight o'clock."

"Then I have no place to go."

He said, "I'll fix up a room for you. Stay in the hotel tonight, and come back." So I stayed in the hotel. Next day I went there at twelve o'clock, tired. They were eating. They gave me lunch. For the first time I had a real meal. I had lost even the appetite for food. I didn't know what hunger was or what thirst was.

After lunch the Swami called me and said, "I am looking for a man exactly like you. My assistant who was doing the editorial work is mentally ill—he has ended up in the hospital. I have to bring out this Vivekananda Centenary number. You are the right man for me to have at this time. You can help me."

I said, "I can't write anything. Maybe I did editing in those days, but now I can't do anything. I'm a finished man. I can't be of any help in that direction."

He said, "No, no, no, together we can do something." He was very badly in need of someone with a background in Indian philosophy and everything. He could have had anybody he wanted, but he said, "No, no, no, it is all right. Rest for some time, stay here, I'll take care of you."

I said, "I don't want to do literary work. Give me a room, and I will wash your dishes or do something, but that kind of work I am singularly incapable of."

He said, "No, no, no, I want that." So I tried to do something—not to my satisfaction, not to his satisfaction—but somehow together we brought out the issue.

He was also giving me money—five pounds, like all the other swamis. For the first time I had five pounds to spend. So, "What to do with this?" I had lost the sense of the value of money because I'd had no money. There was a time when I could write a check for one hundred thousand rupees. After some time, not even one paisa in my pocket—now five pounds. "What am I to do with this?" So, I decided to see every movie in London with that money. I used to stay at the mission and do work in the morning, eat there at one o'clock and go off to a movie. There came a time when I could not find any movie to see. In the London outskirts they used to show three movies for one shilling, or something like that, so I exhausted all the movies and spent all that money.

I used to sit there in the meditation room, wondering at these people meditating: "Why are they doing all those silly things?" By this time the whole thing had gone out of my system. But I had a very strange experience in that meditation center. Whatever it was—my own projection or something—the facts are there. For the first time I felt something peculiar. I was sitting, doing nothing, looking at all those people, pitying them. "These people are meditating. Why do they want to go in for samadhi? They are not going to get anything. I have been through all that. They are kidding themselves. What can I do to save them from wasting all their lives doing all that kind of thing? It is not going to lead them anywhere." I was sitting there—nothing, blankness—when I felt something very strange. There was some kind of a movement inside of my body. Suddenly I found something was moving. Some energy was coming out from the penis and through my head as if there was a hole. It was moving in circles in the clockwise direction, and then in the anticlockwise direction. It was like the Wills cigarette advertisement at the airport. It was such a funny thing for me, but I didn't relate this to anything at all. I was a finished man. Somebody was feeding me, somebody was taking care of me, there was no thought of the morrow. Yet inside of me there was some kind of a thing. "It is a perverse way of living. It is perversity carried to its extremity. This is not anything." But yet, the head was missing. What could I do? It went on and on and on. After three months I said, "I'm going. I can't do this kind of thing." Towards the end the Swami gave me some money, forty or fifty pounds. Then I decided.

You see, I still had an airline ticket to return to India. So I went to Paris, turned in the ticket and made some money because it was paid in dollars. With this thirty-five pounds I think I had about a hundred and fifty pounds. For three months I lived in Paris in some hotel, wandering in the streets as I had done before. The only difference was that now I had some money in my pocket. But slowly this money disappeared. After three months I decided I must go, but I resisted returning to India. Somehow I didn't want to go to India. Because of my family, the children, I was frightened of returning to India. That would complicate matters. All of them would come to me. I didn't want to go at all; I resisted that. I had had a bank account in Switzerland for years and years. I thought I still had some money there. The last resort was to go to Switzerland and take the money out and then see what happened. So I came out of the hotel and got into a taxi and said, "Take me to the Gare de Lyon." But the trains from Paris to Zurich (where I had my account) go from the Gare de l'Est, so I don't know why I told him to take me to the Gare de Lyon. So, he dropped me at the Gare de Lyon, and I got into the train going to Geneva.

I landed in Geneva with a hundred and fifty francs, or something to spend. I continued to stay in a hotel though I had no money to pay the bill. After two weeks they produced the bill. "Come on, money! What about the bill?" I had no money. I threw up my hands.

The only thing left to me was to go to the Indian Consulate and say, "Send me to India. I am finished, you see." So, the resistance to returning to India was finished, and I went to the Consulate and took out the scrapbook: "One of the most brilliant speakers that India has ever produced," with the opinions of Norman Cousins and Radhakrishnan about my talents.

The Vice-Consul said, "We can't send this kind of man to India at the expense of the Government of India. What do you think? Try and get some money from India, and in the meantime come and stay with me." So, you see, it went on and on and on. There I met this Swiss lady [Valentine de Kerven]. She was the translator at the Indian Consulate, but that day she happened to be there at the reception desk because the receptionist was absent or something. We started talking, and then we became close friends.

She said, "If you want to stay, I can arrange for you to stay in Switzerland. If you don't want to go to India, don't go." After one month the Consulate sent me away, but we managed. She created a home for me in Switzerland. She gave up her job. She is not rich. She has just a little money, her pension, but we could live on this money.

So, we went to Saanen. That place has some significance to me. I had been there in '53 while traveling through that area, and when I saw this place, something in me said, "Get off the train and spend some time here." So I spent one week there in 1953. I said to myself, "This is the place where I must spend the rest of my life." I had plenty of money then, but my wife didn't want to stay in Switzerland, because of the climate. Many other things happened, and we went to America. So this unfulfilled dream materialized. Valentine and I went to Saanen because I had always wanted to live there. So I continue to live there. Then J. Krishnamurti chose Saanen, for some reason or other, for his meetings every summer. This chap started coming to Saanen. I lived there; I was not interested in Krishnamurti or anything. I was not interested in anything. For example, Valentine lived with me for a few years before my forty-ninth year. She can tell you that I never talked of this at all to her—my interest in truth, reality—nothing. I never discussed this subject with her at all, or with anybody else. There was no search in me, no seeking after something, but something funny was going on.

During that time (I call it the "incubation") all kinds of things were happening to me inside—headaches, constant headaches, terrible pains here in the brain. I swallowed I don't know how many tens of thousands of aspirins. Nothing gave me relief. It was not migraine or any of those known headaches, but tremendous headaches. Those aspirin pills and fifteen to twenty cups of coffee every day to free myself! One day Valentine said, "What! You are taking fifteen cups of coffee every day. Do you know what it means in terms of money? It is three or four hundred francs per month. What is this?" Anyway, it was such a terrible thing for me.

All kinds of funny things happened to me. I remember when I rubbed my body like this, there was a sparkle, like a phosphorous glow, on the body. She used to run out of her bedroom to see. She thought there were cars going that way in the middle of the night. Every time I rolled in my bed there was a sparkling of light, and it was so funny for me. "What is this?" It was electricity; that is why I say it is an electromagnetic field. At first I thought it was because of my nylon clothes and static electricity, but then I stopped using nylon. I was a very skeptical heretic, to the tips of my toes. I never believed in anything. Even if I saw some miracle happen before me, I didn't accept that at all. Such was the make-up of this man. It never occurred to me that anything of that sort was in the making for me.

Very strange things happened to me, but I never related those things to liberation or freedom or moksha, because by that time the whole thing had gone out of my system. I had arrived at a point where I said to myself, "Buddha deluded himself and deluded others. All those teachers and saviors of mankind were damned fools—they fooled themselves. So I'm not interested in this kind of thing anymore." So it went out of my system completely. It went on and on in its own way— peculiar things. But never did I say to myself, "Well, I am getting there, I am nearer to that." There is no nearness to that, there is no faraway-ness from that, there is no closeness to that. Nobody is nearer to that because he is different, he is prepared. There's no readiness for that. It just hits you like a ton of bricks.

Then [April 1967] I happened to be in Paris when J. Krishnamurti also happened to be there. Some of my friends suggested, "Why don't you go and listen to your old friend? He is here giving a talk."

"All right, I haven't heard him for so many years—almost twenty years. Let me go and listen." When I got there they demanded two francs from me. I said, "I am not ready to pay two francs to listen to J. Krishnamurti. No, come on, let us go and do something foolish. Let's go to a strip-tease joint, the Folies Bergere or the Casino de Paris. Come on, let us go there for twenty francs." So, there we were at the Casino de Paris watching the show. I had a very strange experience at that time. I didn't know whether I was the dancer or whether there was some other dancer dancing on the stage. A very strange experience for me— a peculiar kind of movement here, inside of me. (This is now some-thing natural for me.) There was no division; there was nobody who was looking at the dancer. The question of whether I was the dancer, or whether there was a dancer out there on the stage, puzzled me. This kind of peculiar experience of the absence of division between me and the dancer puzzled me and bothered me for some time. Then we came out.

The question "What is that state?" had a tremendous intensity for me, not an emotional intensity. The more I tried to find an answer, the more I failed to find an answer, the more intensity the question had. It's like (I always give this simile) rice chaff. If a heap of rice chaff is ignited, it continues burning inside. You don't see any fire outside, but when you touch it, it burns you of course. In exactly the same way the question was going on and on and on: "What is that state?" I want it. Finished. Krishnamurti said, "You have no way," but still I want to know what that state is, the state in which Buddha was, Sankara was, and all those teachers were.

Then [July 1967] there arrived another phase. Krishnamurti was again there in Saanen giving talks. My friends dragged me there and said, "Now at least it is a free business. Why don't you come and listen?"

I said, "All right, I'll come and listen." When I listened to him, something funny happened to me—a peculiar kind of feeling that he was describing my state and not his state. Why did I want to know his state?

He was describing something, some movements, some awareness, some silence. "In that silence there is no mind; there is action." All kinds of things. So, "I am in that state. What the hell have I been doing these thirty or forty years, listening to all these people and struggling, wanting to understand his state or the state of somebody else, Buddha or Jesus? I am in that state. Now I am in that state." So, then I walked out of the tent and never looked back.

Then—very strange—that question, "What is that state?" transformed itself into another question: "How do I know that I am in that state, the state of Buddha, the state I very much wanted and demanded from everybody? I am in that state, but how do I know?"

The next day [UG's forty-ninth birthday] I was sitting on a bench under a tree overlooking one of the most beautiful spots in the whole world, the seven hills and seven valleys [of Saanenland]. I was sitting there. Not that the question was there. The whole of my being was that question: "How do I know that I am in that state? There is some kind of peculiar division inside of me. There is somebody who knows that he is in that state. The knowledge of that state—what I have read, what I have experienced, what they have talked about—it is this knowledge that is looking at that state. So it is only this knowledge that has projected that state." I said to myself, "Look here, old chap, after forty years you have not moved one step. You are there in square number one. It is the same knowledge that projected your mind there when you asked this question. You are in the same situation asking the same question, "How do I know?" Because it is this knowledge, the description of the state by those people, that has created this state for you. You are kidding yourself. You are a damned fool." So, nothing. But still there was some kind of a peculiar feeling that this was the state.

The second question, "How do I know that this is the state?"—I did-
n't have any answer for that question. It was like a question in a
whirlpool. It went on and on and on. Then suddenly the question disappeared. Nothing happened; the question just disappeared. I didn't
say to myself, "Oh, my God! Now I have found the answer." Even that
state disappeared—the state I thought I was in, the state of Buddha,
Jesus. Even that has disappeared. The question has disappeared. The
whole thing is finished for me, and that's all, you see. From then on,
never did I say to myself, "Now I have the answer to all those questions." That state of which I had said, "This is the state"—that state
disappeared. The question disappeared. Finished, you see. It is not
emptiness; it is not blankness; it is not the void. It is not any of those
things. The question disappeared suddenly, and that is all.

[The disappearance of his fundamental question, on discovering that
it had no answer, was a physiological phenomenon. UG says it was "a
sudden 'explosion' inside, blasting, as it were, every cell, every nerve,
and every gland in my body." And with that explosion, the illusion that
there is continuity of thought, that there is a center, an "I" linking up
the thoughts, was not there any more.]

Then thought cannot link up. The linking gets broken, and once it
is broken, it is finished. Then it is not once that thought explodes;
every time a thought arises, it explodes. So, this continuity comes to an
end, and thought falls into its natural rhythm.

Since then I have no questions of any kind, because the questions
cannot stay there any more. The only questions I have are very simple
questions ("How do I go to Hyderabad?" for example) to function in
this world. And people have answers for these questions. For those
other questions, nobody has any answers, so there are no questions any
more.

Everything in the head has tightened. There was no room for anything there inside of my brain. For the first time I became conscious of
my head with everything "tight" inside of it. So, these vasanas [past
impressions] or whatever you call them—they do try to show their
heads sometimes, but then the brain cells are so tight that they have no
opportunity to fool around there any more. The division cannot stay
there. It's a physical impossibility; you don't have to do a thing about
it, you see. That is why I say that when this "explosion" takes place (I
use the word *explosion* because it's like a nuclear explosion) it leaves

behind chain reactions. Every cell in your body, the cells in the very marrow of your bones, have to undergo this change—I don't want to use that word. It's an irreversible change. There's no question of your going back. There's no question of a fall for this man at all. Irreversible—an alchemy of some sort.

It is like a nuclear explosion, you see. It shatters the whole body. It is not an easy thing. It is the end of the man—such a shattering thing that it blasts every cell, every nerve in your body. I went through terrible physical torture at that moment. Not that you experience the explosion; you can't experience the explosion. But its after-effect, the fall-out, is the thing that changes the whole chemistry of your body.

Sir, you must have experienced, if I may use the words, higher planes.

You are talking of planes? There are no planes—no planes, no levels. You see, there is one very strange thing that happens as a result of this explosion or whatever you want to call it. At no time does the thought that I am different from you come into this consciousness. Never. Never does that thought come into my consciousness and tell me that you are different from me or I am different from you, because there is no point here, there is no center here. Only with reference to this center do you create all the other points.

In some way, you must certainly be different from other people.

Physiologically, probably.

You said that tremendous chemical changes have taken place in you. How do you know this? Were you ever examined, or is this an inference?

The after-effects of that explosion, the way the senses are operating now without any coordinator or center—that's all I can say. Another thing—the chemistry has changed. I can say that because unless that alchemy or change in the whole chemistry takes place, there is no way of freeing this organism from thought, from the continuity of thought. So, since there is no continuity of thought, you can very easily say that something has happened, but what actually has happened? I have no way of experiencing this at all.

It may be that the mind is playing games and that one merely thinks one is an "exploded man."

I am not trying to sell anything here. It is impossible for you to simulate this. This is a thing that has happened outside the field, the area, in which I expected, dreamed, and wanted change, so I don't call this a change. I really don't know what has happened to me. What I am telling you is the way I am functioning. There seems to be some difference between the way you are functioning and the way I am functioning, but basically there can't be any difference. How can there be any difference between you and me? There can't be; but from the way we are trying to express ourselves, there seems to be. I have the feeling that there is some difference, and what that difference is, is all that I am trying to understand. So, this is the way I am functioning.

[UG noticed, during the week following the explosion, fundamental changes in the functioning of his senses. On the last day his body went through "a process of physical death," and the changes became permanent features.]

Then began the changes—from the next day onwards, for seven days—every day one change. First I discovered the softness of the skin, the blinking of the eyes stopped, and then changes in taste, smell and hearing. These five changes I noticed. Maybe they were there even before, and I only noticed them for the first time.

On the first day I noticed that my skin was soft like silk and had a peculiar kind of glow, a golden color. I was shaving, and each time I tried to shave, the razor slipped. I changed blades, but it was no use. I touched my face. My sense of touch was different, you see, also the way I held the razor. Especially my skin—my skin was soft as silk and had this golden glow. I didn't relate this to anything at all; I just observed it.

On the second day I became aware for the first time that my mind was in what I call a declutched state. I was upstairs in the kitchen and Valentine had prepared tomato soup. I looked at it, and I didn't know what it was. She told me it was tomato soup, and I tasted it, and I recognized, "This is how tomato soup tastes." Then I swallowed the soup, and then I returned to this odd frame of mind—though "frame of mind" is not the phrase for it. It was a frame of "not mind" in which I forgot again. I asked again, "What is that?" Again she said it was tomato soup. Again I tasted it. Again I swallowed and forgot. I played with this for some time. It was such a funny business for me then, this declutched state; now it has become normal. I no longer spend time in reverie, worry, conceptualization and the other kinds of thinking that most people do when they're alone. My mind is only engaged when it's needed, for instance when you ask questions, or when I have to fix the tape-recorder or something like that. The rest of the time my mind is in the declutched state. Of course now I have my memory back. I lost it at first, but now I have it back. But my memory is in the background and only comes into play when it's needed, automatically. When it's not needed, there is no mind here. There is no thought; there is only life.

On the third day some friends invited themselves over for dinner, and I said, "All right, I'll prepare something." But somehow I couldn't smell or taste properly. I became gradually aware that these two senses had been transformed. Every time some odor entered my nostrils it irritated my olfactory center in just about the same way, whether it came from the most expensive scent or from cow dung. It was the same irritation. And then, every time I tasted something, I tasted the dominant ingredient only. The taste of the other ingredients came slowly after. From that moment perfume made no sense to me, and spicy food had no appeal for me. I could taste only the dominant spice, the chili or whatever it was.

On the fourth day something happened to the eyes. We were sitting in the Rialto restaurant, and I became aware of a tremendous sort of "vista vision," like a concave mirror. Things coming towards me, moved into me, as it were, and things going away from me, seemed to move from inside me. It was such a puzzle to me. It was as if my eyes were a gigantic camera, changing focus without my doing anything. Now I am used to the puzzle. Nowadays that is how I see. When you drive me around in your Mini, I am like a cameraman dollying along. The cars in the other direction go into me, and the cars that pass us come out of me, and when my eyes fix on something they fix on it with total attention, like a camera. Another thing about my eyes: When we came back from the restaurant I came home and looked in the mirror to see what was odd about my eyes, to see how they were "fixed." I looked in the mirror for a long time, and then I observed that my eyelids were not blinking. For half an hour or forty-five minutes I looked into the mirror—still no blinking of the eyes. Instinctive blinking was over for me, and it still is.

On the fifth day I noticed a change in hearing. When I heard the barking of a dog, the barking originated inside me. And the same with the mooing of the cow, the whistle of the train—suddenly all sounds originated inside me, as it were, coming from within, and not from outside. They still do.

Five senses changed in five days, and on the sixth day I was lying down on a sofa. Valentine was there in the kitchen. Suddenly my body disappeared. There was no body there. I looked at my hand. (Crazy thing—you would certainly put me in the mental hospital.) I looked at it. "Is this my hand?" There was no questioning here, but the whole situation was like that. That is all I am describing. So I touched this body—nothing. I didn't feel there was anything there except the touch, you see, the point of contact. Then I called Valentine. "Do you see my body on this sofa? Nothing inside of me says that this is my body."

She touched it. "This is your body." And yet that assurance didn't give me any comfort or satisfaction.

"What is this funny business? My body is missing." My body had gone away, and it has never come back. The points of contact are all that is there for the body—nothing else is there for me—because the seeing is altogether independent of the sense of touch here. So it is not possible for me to create a complete image of my body even, because where there's no sense of touch there are missing points here in the consciousness.

On the seventh day I was again lying on the same sofa, relaxing, enjoying the declutched state. Valentine would come in, I would recognize her as Valentine; she would go out of the room—finish, blank, no Valentine. "What is this? I can't even imagine what Valentine looks like." I would listen to the sounds coming from inside me. I could not relate. I had discovered that all my senses were without any coordinating thing inside. The coordinator was missing.

I felt something happening inside of me—the life energy drawing to a focal point from different parts of my body. I said to myself, "Now you have come to the end of your life. You are going to die." Then I called Valentine and said, "I am going to die, Valentine, and you will have to do something with this body. Hand it over to the doctors—maybe they will use it. I don't believe in burning or burial or any of those things. In your own interest you have to dispose of this body—one day it will stink. So, why not give it away?"

She said, "You are a foreigner. The Swiss government won't take your body. Forget about it." Then she went away. And then there was this whole business of the frightening movement of the life force coming to a point, as it were. I was lying down on the sofa. Her bed was empty, so I moved over to that bed and stretched myself, getting ready. She ignored me and went away. She said, "One day you say this thing has changed, another day this thing has changed, a third day this thing has changed. What is this whole business?" She was not interested in any of those things. Never was she interested in any of these religious matters—never heard of those things. "You say you are going to die. You are not going to die. You are all right, hale and healthy." She went away. Then I stretched myself, and this was going on and on and on. The whole life energy was moving to some focal point. Where it was, I don't know. Then a point arrived where the whole thing looked as if the aperture of a camera was trying to close itself. (It is the only simile that I can think of. The way I am describing this is quite different from the way things happened at that time, because there was nobody there thinking in such terms. All this was part of my experience, otherwise I wouldn't be able to talk about it.) So, the aperture was trying to close itself, and something was there trying to keep it open. Then after a while there was no will to do anything, not even to prevent the aperture closing itself. Suddenly, as it were, it closed. I don't know what happened after that.

This process lasted for forty-nine minutes—this process of dying. It was like a physical death, you see. Even now it happens to me. The hands and feet become so cold, the body becomes stiff, the heartbeat slows down, the breathing slows down, and then there is a gasping for breath. Up to a point you are there, you breathe your last breath, as it were, and then you are finished. What happens after that, nobody knows.

When I came out of that, somebody said there was a telephone call for me. I came out and went downstairs to answer it. I was in a daze. I didn't know what had happened. It was a physical death. What brought me back to life, I don't know. How long it lasted, I don't know. I can't say anything about that, because the experiencer was finished. There was nobody to experience that death at all. So, that was the end of it. I got up.

I didn't feel that I was a new-born baby—no question of enlightenment at all. But the things that had astonished me that week, the changes in taste, seeing and so on, had become permanent fixtures. I call all these events the "calamity." I call it the calamity because from the point of view of one who thinks this is something fantastic, blissful, full of beatitude, love, ecstasy and all that kind of thing, this is physical torture. This is a calamity from that point of view. Not a calamity to me, but a calamity to those who have an image that something marvelous is going to happen. It's something like this: you imagine New York, you dream about it, you want to be there. When you are actually there, nothing of it is there. It is a godforsaken place, and even the devils have probably forsaken that place. It's not the thing that you had sought after and wanted so much, but totally different. What is there, you really don't know—you have no way of knowing anything about that. There is no image here. In that sense I can never tell myself or anybody, "I'm an enlightened man, a liberated man, a free man. I'm going to liberate mankind." Free from what? How can I liberate somebody else? There's no question of liberating anybody. For that, I must have an image that I am a free man, you understand?

Then, on the eighth day I was sitting on the sofa and suddenly there was an outburst of tremendous energy—tremendous energy shaking the whole body, and along with the body, the sofa, the chalet and the whole universe, as it were—shaking, vibrating. You can't create that movement at all. It was sudden. Whether it was coming from outside or inside, from below or above, I don't know. I couldn't locate the spot; it was all over. It lasted for hours and hours. I couldn't bear it but there was nothing I could do to stop it. There was a total helplessness. This went on and on, day after day, day after day. Whenever I sat it started—this vibration like an epileptic fit or something. It went on for days and days.

[For three days UG lay on his bed, his body contorted with pain. It was, he says, as if he felt pain in every cell of his body, one after the other. Similar outbursts of energy occurred intermittently throughout the next six months, whenever he lay down or relaxed.]

The body feels the pain. That's a very painful process. Very painful. It is a physical pain because the body has limitations. It has a form, a shape of its own. So when there is an outburst of energy, which is not your energy or my energy or God's (or call it by any name you like), it is like a river in spate. The energy that is operating there does not feel the limitations of the body. It is not interested; it has its own momentum. It is a very painful thing. It is not that ecstatic, blissful beatitude and all that rubbish—stuff and nonsense! It is really a painful thing. Oh, I suffered for months and months after that—before that too. Everybody has. Even Ramana Maharshi suffered after that.

A great cascade—not one, but thousands of cascades. It went on and on and on for months and months. It's a very painful experience—painful in the sense that the energy has a peculiar operation of its own. There is an atom: lines going like that. [UG demonstrates.] It is clockwise, counter-clockwise, and then it is this way, and then this way, and then this way. Like an atom it moves inside—not in one part of your body, the whole body. It is as if a wet towel were being wrung to get rid of the water. It is like that, the whole of our body. It's such a painful thing. It goes on even now. You can't invite it; you can't ask it to come; you can't do anything. It gives you the feeling that it is enveloping you, that it is descending on you. Descending from where? Where is it coming from? How is it coming? Every time it is new—very strange. Every time it comes in a different way, so you don't know what is happening. You lie down on your bed, and suddenly it begins. It begins to move slowly like ants. I'd think there were bugs in my bed, jump out, look— no bugs—then I'd go back—then again. [laughs] The hairs are electrified, so it slowly moves.

There were pains all over the body. Thought has controlled this body to such an extent that when that loosens, the whole metabolism is agog. The whole thing was changing in its own way without my doing anything. And then the movement of the hands changed. Usually your hands turn this way. [UG demonstrates.] Here, this wrist joint had terrible pains for six months until it turned itself, and all the movements are now like this. That is why they say my movements are mudras [mystical gestures]. The movements of the hands are quite different now than before. Then there were pains in the marrow of the bones. Every cell started changing, and it went on and on for six months.

And then the sex hormones started changing. I didn't know whether I was a man or a woman. "What is this business?" Suddenly there was a breast on the left-hand side. All kinds of things—I don't want to go into details. There is a complete record of all these things. It went on and on and on. It took three years for this body to fall into a new rhythm of its own.

Can we understand how it happened to you?

No.

Can we understand what happened?

You can read a description of the events of my life, that's all. One day, around my forty-ninth birthday something stopped. Another day another sense changed; the third day something else changed. There is a record of the way the things happened to me. What value has that to you? It has no value at all. On the other hand it's very dangerous because you try to simulate the outward manifestations. People simulate these things and believe that something is happening. That's what these people do. I behaved normally. I didn't know what was happening. It was a strange situation. There is no point in leaving any record. People will only simulate these things. The state is something natural.

[Up and down his torso, neck, and head, at those points that Indian holy men call chakras, his friends observed swellings of various shapes and colors, which came and went at intervals. On his lower abdomen the swellings were horizontal, cigar-shaped bands. Above the navel was a hard, almond-shaped swelling. A hard, blue swelling, like a large medallion, in the middle of his chest was surmounted by another smaller, brownish-red, medallion-shaped swelling at the base of his throat. These two "medallions" were as though suspended from a vari-colored, swollen ring—blue, brownish and light yellow—around his neck, as in pictures of the Hindu gods. There were also other similarities between the swellings and the depictions of Indian religious art. His throat was swollen to a shape that made his chin seem to rest on the head of a cobra, as in the traditional images of Siva. Just above the bridge of the nose was a white lotus-shaped swelling. All over the head the small blood vessels expanded, forming patterns like the stylized lumps on the heads of Buddha statues. Like the horns of Moses and the Taoist mystics, two large, hard swellings periodically came and went. The arteries in his neck expanded and rose, blue and snake-like, into his head.]

I do not want to be an exhibitionist, but you are doctors. There is something to the symbolism they have in India—the cobra. Do you see the swellings here? They take the shape of a cobra. Yesterday was the new moon. The body is affected by everything that is happening around you. It is not separate from what is happening around you. Whatever is happening there is also happening here; there is only the physical response. This is affection. You can't prevent this, for the simple reason that the armor that you have built around yourself is destroyed, so it is very vulnerable to everything that is happening there. With the phases of the moon—full moon, half moon, quarter moon—these swellings here take the shape of a cobra. Maybe that is the reason why some people have created all these images—Siva and all those kinds of things. But why should it take the shape of a cobra? I have asked many doctors why this swelling is here, but nobody could give me a satisfactory answer. I don't know if there are any glands or anything here.

This I have discussed so many times with doctors who are doing research into the ductless glands. Those glands are what the Hindus call chakras. These ductless glands are located in exactly the same spots where the Hindus speculated the chakras are. There is one gland here that is called the thymus gland. That is very active when you are a child—very active. They have feelings, extraordinary feelings. When you reach the age of puberty it becomes dormant—that's what they say. When again this kind of a thing happens, when you are reborn again, that gland is automatically activated, so all the feelings are there. Feelings are not thoughts, not emotions. You feel for somebody. If somebody hurts himself there, that hurt is felt here—not as a pain, but there is a feeling, you see. You automatically say, "Ah!"

This actually happened to me when I was staying in a coffee plantation. A mother started beating a child, a little child, you know. She was mad, hopping mad, and she hit the child so hard, the child almost turned blue. And somebody asked me, "Why did you not interfere and stop her?" I was standing there. I was so puzzled, you see. "Who should I take pity on, the mother or the child?" That was my answer. "Who is responsible?" Both were in a ridiculous situation. The mother could not control her anger, and the child was so helpless and innocent. This went on—it was moving from one to the other—and then I found all those things [marks] on my back. So I was also part of that. I am not saying this just to claim something. That is possible because conscious-ness cannot be divided. Anything that is happening there is affecting you. This is affection, you understand? There is no question of your sit-ting in judgment on anybody. The situation happens to be that, so you are affected by that. You are affected by everything that is happening there.

In the entire universe?

That is too big, you see. Anything that is happening within your field of consciousness. Consciousness is, of course, not limited. If he is hurt there, you also are hurt here. If you are hurt, there is an immediate response there. I can't say about the universe, the whole universe, but in your field of consciousness, in the limited field in which you are operating at that particular moment, you are responding—not that *you* are responding.

There are so many glands here—for example, the pituitary—third eye, ajña chakra, they call it. When once the interference of thought is finished, it is taken over by this gland. It is this gland that gives the instructions or orders to the body, not thought any more. Thought cannot interfere. (That is why they call it that, probably. [The literal meaning of ajña is *command*.] I'm not interpreting or any such thing; perhaps this gives you an idea.) But you have built an armor, created an armor, with this thought, and you don't allow yourself to be affected by things.

Since there is nobody who uses this thought as a self-protective mechanism, it burns itself up. Thought undergoes combustion, ioniza-tion (if I may use your scientific term). Thought is, after all, vibration. So, when this kind of ionization of thought takes place, it throws out, sometimes it covers the whole body with, an ash-like substance. Your body is covered with that when there is no need for thought at all. When you don't use it, what happens to that thought? It burns itself out—that is the energy. It's a combustion. The body gets heated, you know. There is tremendous heat in the body as a result of this, and so the skin is covered—your face, your feet, everything—with this ash-like substance.

That's one of the reasons why I express it in pure and simple physi-cal and physiological terms. It has no psychological content at all, it has no mystical content, it has no religious overtones at all, as I see it. I am bound to say that, and I don't care whether you accept it or not. It is of no importance to me.

This kind of thing must have happened to so many people. I say this happens to one in a billion, and you are that one in a billion. It is not something that one is specially prepared for. There are no purificatory methods necessary. There is no sadhana necessary for this kind of thing to happen—no preparation of any kind. The consciousness is so pure that whatever you are doing in the direction of purifying that consciousness is adding impurity to it.

Consciousness has to flush itself out. It has to purge itself of every trace of holiness, every trace of unholiness, everything. Even what you consider sacred and holy is a contamination in that consciousness. It is not through any volition of yours. When once the frontiers are broken—not through any effort or volition of yours—then the floodgates are open and everything goes out. In that process of flushing out, you have all these visions. It's not a vision outside there or inside of you. Suddenly you yourself, the whole consciousness, takes the shape of Buddha, Jesus, Mahavira, Mohammed, Socrates—only those people who have come into this state, not great men, not the leaders of mankind—it is very strange—but only those people to whom this kind of thing happened.

One of them was some kind of a colored man, and during that time I could tell people how he looked. Then some woman with breasts, flowing hair—naked. I was told that there were two saints here in India—Akkamahadevi and Lalleswari—they were women, naked women. Suddenly you have these two breasts, the flowing hair—even the organs change into female organs.

But still there is a division there—you, and the form the consciousness has assumed, the form of Buddha, say, or Jesus Christ or God knows what. The same situation: "How do I know I am in that state?" But that division cannot stay long; it disappears and something else comes. Probably something happened to so many hundreds of people. This is part of history—so many rishis, some Westerners, monks, so many women, and sometimes very strange things. You see, all that people have experienced before you is part of your consciousness. I use the expression "the saints go marching out." In Christianity they have a hymn, "When the Saints Go Marching In." They run out of your consciousness because they cannot stay there any more, because all that is impurity, a contamination there.

You can say (I can't make any definite statement) probably it is because of the impact on the human consciousness of the explosions of all those saints, sages, and saviors of mankind that there is this dissatisfaction in you, that whatever is there is all the time trying to burst out, as it were. Maybe that is so; I can't say anything about it. You can say that they are there because they are pushing you to this point, and once the purpose is achieved they have finished their job and they go away. That is only speculation on my part. But this flushing out of everything good and bad, holy and unholy, sacred and profane, has got to happen. Otherwise your consciousness is still contaminated, still impure. During that time it goes on and on and on—there are hundreds and thousands of them. Then, you see, you are put back into that primeval, primordial state of consciousness. Once it has become pure, of and by itself, then nothing can touch it, nothing can contaminate that any more. All the past up to that point is there, but it cannot influence your actions any more.

All these visions and everything were happening for three years after the calamity. Now the whole thing is finished. The divided state of consciousness cannot function at all any more. It is always in the undivided state of consciousness—nothing can touch that. Anything can happen—the thought can be a good thought, a bad thought, the telephone number of a London prostitute. During my wanderings in London, I used to look at those telephone numbers fixed to the trees. I was not interested in going to the prostitute, but those things, the numbers, interested me. I had nothing else to do, no books to read, nothing to do but look at those numbers. One number gets fixed in there, it comes there, it repeats itself. It doesn't matter what comes there—good, bad, holy, unholy. Who is there to say, "This is good; that is bad"? The whole thing is finished. That is why I have to use the phrase *religious experience* (not in the sense in which you use the word *religion*). It puts you back to the source. You are back in that primeval, primordial, pure state of consciousness—call it awareness or whatever you like. In that state things are happening, and there is nobody who is interested, nobody who is looking at them. They come and go in their own way, like the Ganges water flowing. The sewerage water comes in, half-burnt corpses, both good things and bad things—everything—but that water is always pure.

The most puzzling and bewildering part of the whole thing was when the sensory activities began their independent careers. There was no coordinator linking the senses, so we had terrible problems. Valentine had to go through the whole business. We'd go for a walk, and I'd look at a flower and ask, "What is that?"

She'd say, "That is a flower."

I'd take a few more steps, look at a cow and ask, "What is that?" Like a baby, I had to relearn everything all over (not actually relearn, but all the knowledge was in the background and never came to the forefront, you see). "What is this crazy business?" I have to put it in words—not that I felt I was in a crazy state. I was a very sane man, acting sanely, everything going on, and yet this ridiculous business of asking about everything. "What is this? What is that?" That's all; no other questions. Valentine also didn't know what to make out of the whole business. She even went to a leading psychiatrist in Geneva. She rushed to him. She wanted to understand, but at the same time she felt that there was nothing crazy about me. If I'd done one crazy thing she would have left me. Never. Only strange things, you see. "What is that?"

"That is a cow."

"What is that?"

"That is that." It went on and on and on, and it was too much for her and too much for me.

When she met the psychiatrist, he said, "Unless we see the person, we can't tell anything. Bring him." But I knew that something really fantastic had happened inside. What it was, I didn't know, but that didn't bother me. "Why ask if that's a cow? What's the difference whether it is a cow, a donkey or a horse?" That bewildering situation continued for a long time. All the knowledge was in the background. It's the same situation even now, but I don't ask those questions any more. When I am looking at something, I really don't know what I'm looking at. That is why I say it is a state of not knowing. I really don't know. That is why I say that once you are there, through some luck, some strange chance, from then on everything happens in its own way. You are always in a state of samadhi; there is no question of going in and out of it; you are always there. I don't want to use that word, so I say it is a state of not knowing. You really don't know what you are looking at.

I can't do anything about it. There is no question of my going back or anything; it is all finished. It is operating and functioning in a different way. (I have to use the words *different way* to give you a feel about it.)

There seems to be some difference. You see, my difficulty with the people who come to see me is this: they don't seem to be able to understand the way I am functioning, and I don't seem to be able to understand the way they are functioning. How can we carry on a dialogue? Both of us have to stop. How can there be a dialogue between us both? I am talking like a raving maniac. All my talking totally unrelated, just like a maniac's—the difference is only a hair's breadth. That is why I say you either flip or fly at that moment.

There is no difference, absolutely no difference. Somehow, you see, by some luck, by some strange chance, this kind of thing happens (I have to use the word *happens* to give you a feel about that) and the whole thing is finished for you.

Are even those who have "realized" different from one another?

Yes, because the background is different. The background is the only thing that can express itself. What else is there? My expression of it is the background: how I struggled, my path, the path I followed, how I rejected the paths of others. Up to that point I can say what I did or what I did not do, so that did not help me in any way.

But one like you is different from us. We're involved in our thoughts.

He's different, not only from you, but from all the others who are supposed to be in this state, because of his background.

Although everyone who is supposed to have undergone this explosion is unique, in the sense that each one is expressing his own background, there do seem to be some common characteristics.

That is not my concern; it seems to be yours. I never compare myself to somebody else.

And that is all there is to it. My biography is over. There is nothing more to write about, and never will be. If people come and ask me questions, I answer. If they don't, it makes no difference to me. I have not set myself up in the "holy business" of liberating people. I have no particular message for mankind, except to say that all holy systems for obtaining enlightenment are bunk, and that all talk of arriving at a psychological mutation through awareness is poppycock. Psychological mutation is impossible. The natural state can happen only through biological mutation.

Chapter 2

The Mystique of Enlightenment

Compiled by James Brodsky from conversations in
India and Switzerland, 1973

I am not out to liberate anybody. You have to liberate yourself, and you are unable to do that. What I have to say will not do it. I am only interested in describing this state, in clearing away the occultation and mystification in which those people in the "holy business" have shrouded the whole thing. Maybe I can convince you not to waste a lot of time and energy looking for a state that does not exist except in your imagination.

Get this straight, this is your state I am describing, your natural state, not my state or the state of a God-realized man or a mutant or any such thing. This is your natural state, but what prevents what is there from expressing itself in its own way is your reaching out for something, trying to be something other than what you are.

You can never understand this; you can only experience this in terms of your past experience. This is outside the realm of experience. The natural state is acausal; it just happens. No communication is possible, and none necessary. The only thing that is real to you is the way you are functioning. It is an act of futility to relate my description to the way you are functioning. When you stop all this comparison, what is there is your natural state. Then you will not listen to anybody.

There is no teaching of mine, and there never shall be one. *Teaching* is not the word for it. A teaching implies a method or a system, a technique or a new way of thinking to be applied in order to bring about a transformation in your way of life. What I am saying is outside the field of teachability. It is simply a description of the way I am functioning. It is just a description of the natural state of man. This is the way you, stripped of the machinations of thought, are also functioning.

The natural state is not the state of a self-realized, God-realized man. It is not a thing to be achieved or attained. It is not a thing to be willed into existence. It is there. It is the living state. This state is just the functional activity of life. By *life* I do not mean something abstract. It is the life of the senses, functioning naturally without the interference of thought. Thought is an interloper, which thrusts itself into the affairs of the senses. It has a profit motive. Thought directs the activity of the senses to get something out of them, and uses them to give continuity to itself.

Your natural state has no relationship whatsoever with the religious states of bliss, beatitude, and ecstasy. They lie within the field of experience. Those who have led man on his search for religiousness throughout the centuries have perhaps experienced those religious states. So can you. They are thought-induced states of being, and as they come, so do they go. Krishna Consciousness, Buddha Consciousness, Christ Consciousness, or what have you, are all trips in the wrong direction. They are all within the field of time. The timeless can never be experienced, can never be grasped, contained, much less given expression to, by any man. That beaten track will lead you nowhere. There is no oasis situated yonder; you are stuck with the mirage.

This state is a physical condition of your being. It is not some kind of psychological mutation. It is not a state of mind into which you can fall one day, and out of it the next day. You can't imagine the extent to which, as you are now, thought pervades and interferes with the functioning of every cell in your body. Coming into your natural state will blast every cell, every gland, every nerve. It is a chemical change. An alchemy of some sort takes place. But this state has nothing to do with the experiences of chemical drugs such as LSD. Those are experiences; this is not.

Does such a thing as enlightenment exist? To me what does exist is a purely physical process; there is nothing mystical or spiritual about it. If I close the eyes, some light penetrates through the eyelids. If I cover the eyelids, there is still light inside. There seems to be some kind of a hole in the forehead, which doesn't show, but through which something penetrates. In India that light is golden; in Europe it is blue. There is also some kind of light penetration through the back of the neck. It's as if there is a hole running between those spots in the front and back of the skull. There is nothing inside but this light. If you cover those points, there is complete, total darkness. This light doesn't do anything or help the body to function in any way; it's just there.

This state is a state of not knowing. You really don't know what you are looking at. I may look at the clock on the wall for half an hour; still I do not read the time. I don't know it is a clock. All there is inside is wonderment: "What is this that I am looking at?" Not that the question actually phrases itself like that in words. The whole of my being is like a single, big question mark. It is a state of wonder, of wondering, because I just do not know what I am looking at. The knowledge about it—all that I have learned—is held in the background unless there is a demand. It is in the "declutched state." If you ask the time, I will say, "It's a quarter past three" or whatever. It comes quickly like an arrow, then I am back in the state of not knowing, of wonder.

You can never understand the tremendous peace that is always there within you, that is your natural state. Your trying to create a peaceful state of mind is in fact creating disturbance within you. You can only talk of peace, create a state of mind and say to yourself that you are very peaceful. But that is not peace; that is violence. So there is no use in practicing peace, there is no reason to practice silence. Real silence is explosive; it is not the dead state of mind that spiritual seekers think. "Oh, I am at peace with myself! There is silence, a tremendous silence! I experience silence!" That doesn't mean anything at all. Silence is volcanic in its nature. It's bubbling all the time—the energy, the life—that is its quality. You may ask how I know. I don't know. Life is aware of itself, if we can put it that way. It is conscious of itself.

When I talk of feeling, I do not mean the same thing that you do. Actually, feeling is a physical response, a thud in the thymus. The thymus, one of the endocrine glands, is located under the breastbone. The doctors tell us that it is active through childhood until puberty and then becomes dormant. When you come into your natural state, this gland is re-activated. Sensations are felt there. You don't translate them as good or bad; they are just a thud. If there is a movement outside of you—a clock pendulum swinging, or a bird flying across your field of vision—that movement is also felt in the thymus. The whole of your being is that movement or vibrates with that sound; there is no separation. This does not mean that you identify yourself with that bird or whatever: "I am that flying bird." There is no "you" there, nor is there any object. What causes that sensation, you don't know. You do not even know that it is a sensation.

Affection means that you are affected by everything, not that some emotion flows from you towards something. The natural state is a state of great sensitivity, but this is a physical sensitivity of the senses, not some kind of emotional compassion or tenderness for others. There is compassion only in the sense that there are no "others" for me, and so there is no separation.

Is there in you an entity that you call the I or the mind or the self? Is there a coordinator who is coordinating what you are looking at with what you are listening to, what you are smelling with what you are tasting, and so on? Or is there anything that links together the various sensations originating from a single sense—the flow of impulses from the eyes, for example? Actually, there is always a gap between any two sensations. The coordinator bridges that gap; he establishes himself as an illusion of continuity.

In the natural state there is no entity that is coordinating the messages from the different senses. Each sense is functioning independently in its own way. When there is a demand from outside that makes it necessary to coordinate one or two or all of the senses and come up with a response, still there is no coordinator, but there is a temporary state of co-ordination. There is no continuity. When the demand has been met, again there is only the uncoordinated, disconnected, disjointed functioning of the senses. This is always the case. Once the continuity is blown apart—not that it was ever there, but the illusory continuity—it's finished once and for all.

Can this make any sense to you? It cannot. All that you know lies within the framework of your experience, which is of thought. This state is not an experience. I am only trying to give you a feel of it, which is, unfortunately, misleading.

When there is no coordinator, there is no linking of sensations, there is no translating of sensations; they stay pure and simple sensations. I do not even know that they are sensations. I may look at you as you are talking. The eyes will focus on your mouth because that is what is moving, and the ears will receive the sound vibrations. There is nothing inside that links up the two and says that it is you talking. I may be looking at a spring bubbling out of the earth and hear the water, but there is nothing to say that the noise being heard is the sound of water, or that the sound is in any way connected with what I am seeing. I may be looking at my foot, but nothing says that this is my foot. When I am walking, I see my feet moving. It is such a funny thing: "What is that which is moving?"

What functions is a primordial consciousness, untouched by thought.

The eyes are like a very sensitive camera. The physiologists say that light reflected off objects strikes the retina of the eye and the sensation goes through the optic nerve to the brain. The faculty of sight, of seeing, is simply a physical phenomenon. It makes no difference to the eyes whether they are focused on a snow-capped mountain or on a garbage can. They produce sensations in exactly the same way. The eyes look on everyone and everything without discrimination.

You have a feeling that there is a "cameraman" who is directing the eyes. But left to themselves, when there is no cameraman, the eyes do not linger, but are moving all the time. They are drawn by the things outside. Movement attracts them, or brightness or a color that stands out from whatever is around it. There is no "I" looking. Mountains, flowers, trees, cows all look at me. The consciousness is like a mirror, reflecting whatever is there outside. The depth, the distance, the color, everything is there, but there is nobody who is translating these things. Unless there is a demand for knowledge about what I am looking at, there is no separation, no distance from what is there. It may not actually be possible to count the hairs on the head of someone sitting across the room, but there is a kind of clarity that seems as if I could.

The eyes do not blink, except when there is sudden danger. This is something very natural because the things outside are demanding attention all the time. Then, when the eyes are tired, a built-in mechanism in the body cuts them out. They may be open, but they are blurred. But if the eyes stay open all the time, if the reflex action of blinking is not operating, they become dry and you will go blind. So there are some glands beyond the outer corners of the eyes, which are not activated in your case, which act as a watering mechanism. Tears flow all the time from the outer corners. Ignorant people have described them as tears of joy or tears of bliss. There is nothing divine about them. By practicing not blinking, one will not arrive in this state; one will only strain the eyes. And there are neurotics in mental hospitals whose eyes do not blink for one reason or another. For them it is a pathological condition. But once you are in your natural state, by some luck or some strange chance, all this happens in its own way.

Does beauty lie in the eye of the beholder? Does it lie in the object? Where does it lie? Beauty is thought-induced. I do not stop and write poems about the mountain in front of me. What happens is that I am walking and suddenly see something different because the light has changed. I have nothing to do with it. It is not that something new is seen, or that there is a total attention. There has been a sudden change in the light itself. There is no recognition of that as beauty. Clarity is there, which probably wasn't there before the light changed. Then this consciousness suddenly expands to the size of the object in front of the body, and the lungs take a deep breath. This is pranayama [breath control], not what you are doing, sitting in a corner and inhaling through one nostril and exhaling through the other. This pranayama is going on all the time. So, there is consciousness of a sudden change in the breathing, and then it moves on to something else, the mooing of a cow or the howling of a jackal. It is always moving. It does not linger on something that thought has decided is beautiful. There is no one directing.

Do you listen to anybody? You do not; you listen only to yourself. When you leave the sense of hearing alone, all that is there is the vibration of the sound. The words repeat themselves inside of you, as in an echo chamber. This sense is functioning in just the same way with you, except that you think the words you are hearing come from outside of you. Get this straight. You can never hear one word from anyone else, no matter how intimately you think you are in relationship with that person. You hear only your own translations, always. They are all your words you are hearing. All that the other person's words can possibly be to you is a noise, a vibration picked up by the eardrum and transferred to the nerves that run to the brain. You are translating those vibrations all the time, trying to understand, because you want to get something out of what you are hearing. That is all right for a relationship with someone on the level of, "Here is some money; give me a half kilo of carrots," but that is the limit of your relationship, of your communication, with anybody.

When there is no translation, all languages sound the same whether or not your particular knowledge structure speaks a particular language. The only differences are in the spacing of the syllables and in the tune. Languages are melodic in different ways.

It is acquired taste that tells you that Beethoven's Ninth Symphony is more beautiful than a chorus of cats screaming. Both produce equally valid sensations. Of course some sounds can be damaging to the body, and noise levels above a certain number of decibels are hard on the nervous system and can cause deafness. That is not what I am talking about. But the appreciation of music, poetry, and language is all culturally determined and is the product of thought.

Your movement of thought interferes with the process of touch, just as it does with the other senses. Anything you touch is always translated as *hard, soft, warm, cold, wet, dry,* and so on.

You do not realize it, but your thinking creates your own body. Without this thought process there is no body consciousness, which is to say there is no body at all. My body exists for other people; it does not exist for me. There are only isolated points of contact, impulses of touch that are not tied together by thought. So the body is not different from the objects around it. It is a set of sensations like any others. Your body does not belong to you.

Perhaps I can give you the feel of this. I sleep four hours at night, no matter what time I go to bed. Then I lie in bed until morning fully awake. I don't know what is lying there in the bed. I don't know whether I'm lying on my left side or my right side. For hours and hours I lie like this. If there is any noise outside—a bird or something—it just echoes in me. I listen to the "flub-dub-flub-dub" of my heart and don't know what it is. There is no body between the two sheets. The form of the body is not there. If the question, "What is in there?" is asked, there is only an awareness of the points of contact, where the body is in contact with the bed and the sheets, and where it is in contact with itself, at the crossing of the legs, for example. There are only the sensations of touch from these points of contact, and the rest of the body is not there. There is some kind of heaviness, probably the gravitational pull, something very vague. There is nothing inside that links up these things. Even if the eyes are open and looking at the whole body, there are still only the points of contact, and they have no connection with what I am looking at. If I want to try to link up these points of contact into the shape of my own body, probably I will succeed, but by the time it is completed the body is back in the same situation of different points of contact. The linkage cannot stay. It is the same sort of thing when I'm sitting or standing. There is no body.

Can you tell me how mango juice tastes? I can't. You also cannot, but you try to relive the memory of mango juice now. You create for yourself some kind of an experience of how it tastes, which I cannot do. I must have mango juice on my tongue—seeing or smelling it is not enough—to bring that past knowledge into operation and to say, "Yes, this is what mango juice tastes like." This does not mean that personal preferences and tastes change. In a market my hand automatically reaches out for the same items that I have liked all my life. But because I cannot conjure up a mental experience, there can be no craving for foods that are not there.

Smell plays a greater part in your daily life than does taste. The olfactory organs are constantly open to odors. But if you do not interfere with the sense of smell, what is there is only an irritation in the nose. It makes no difference whether you smell cow dung or an expensive French perfume. You rub the nose and move on.

My talking comes out in response to the questions that are asked. I cannot sit and give a talk on the natural state. That is an artificial situation for me. There is nobody who is thinking thoughts and then coming out with answers. When you throw a ball at me, the ball bounces back, and that is what you call an *answer*. But I don't give any answers; this state is expressing itself. I really don't know what I'm saying, and what I'm saying is of no importance. You may transcribe my talking, but it will make no sense to me. It is a dead thing.

What is here, this natural state, is a living thing. It cannot be captured by me, let alone by you. It's like a flower. (This simile is all I can give.) It just blooms. It's there. As long as it is there, it has a fragrance that is different and distinct from that of every other flower. You may not recognize it. You may or may not write odes or sonnets about it. A wandering cow might eat it, or it may be chopped down by a hay cutter, or it fades and is finished. That's the end of it. It's of no importance.

You can't preserve its perfume. Whatever you preserve of this is only a synthetic, a chemical perfume, not the living thing. Preserving the expressions, teachings, or words of such a man has no meaning. This state has only contemporary value, contemporary expression.

The personality does not change when you come into this state. You are, after all, a computer machine, which reacts as it has been programmed. It is in fact your present effort to change yourself that is taking you away from yourself and keeping you from functioning in the natural way. The personality will remain the same. Don't expect such a man to become free from anger or idiosyncrasies. Don't expect some kind of spiritual humility. Such a man may be the most arrogant person you have ever met, because he is touching life at a unique place where no man has touched before.

It is for this reason that each person who comes into this state expresses it in a unique way, in terms relevant to his time. It is also for this reason that if two or more people are living in this state at the same time, they will never get together. They won't dance in the streets hand in hand: "We are all self-realized men! We belong!"

The natural needs of a human being are basic: food, clothing and shelter. You must either work for them or be given them by somebody. If these are your only needs, they are not very difficult to fulfill. To deny yourself the basic needs is not a sign of spirituality; but to require more than food, clothing, and shelter is a neurotic state of mind.

Is not sex a basic human requirement? Sex is dependent upon thought; the body itself has no sex. Only the genitals and perhaps the hormone balances differ between male and female. It is thought that says, "I am a man, and that is a woman, an attractive woman." It is thought that translates sex feelings in the body and says, "These are sexual feelings." And it is thought that provides the build-up without which no sex is possible. "It would be more pleasurable to hold that woman's hand than just to look at her. It would be more pleasurable to kiss her than just to embrace her," and so on. In the natural state there is no build-up of thought. Without that build-up, sex is impossible. And sex is tremendously violent to the body. The body normally is a very peaceful organism, and then you subject it to this tremendous tension and release, which feels pleasurable to you. Actually it is painful to the body.

But through suppression or attempts at sublimation of sex you will never come into this state. As long as you think of God, you will have thoughts of sex. Ask any religious seeker you may know who practices celibacy, whether he doesn't dream of women at night. The peak of the sex experience is the one thing in life you have that comes close to being a first-hand experience. All of the rest of your experiences are second-hand, somebody else's. Why do you weave so many taboos and ideas around this? Why do you destroy the joy of sex? Not that I am advocating indulgence or promiscuity, but through abstinence and continence you will never achieve a thing.

There must be a living contact. If you walk out of the room, you disappear from my consciousness. Where you are, or why you are not here—these questions do not arise. There are no images here; there is no room for them. The sensory apparatus is completely occupied with the things I am looking at now. There must be a living contact with those things that are in the room, not thoughts about things that are not here. And so, if you are totally tuned in to the sensory activity, there is no room for fears about who will feed you tomorrow, or for speculation about God, Truth, and Reality.

This is not a state of omniscience, wherein all of man's eternal questions are answered. Rather, it is a state in which the questioning has stopped. It has stopped because those questions have no relation to the way the organism is functioning, and the way the organism is functioning leaves no room for those questions.

The body has an extraordinary mechanism for renewing itself. This is necessary because the senses in the natural state are functioning at the peak of their sensitivity all the time. So, when the senses become tired, the body goes through death. This is real physical death, not some mental state. It can happen one or more times a day. You do not decide to go through this death; it descends upon you. It feels at first as if you have been given an anesthetic. The senses become increasingly dull, the heartbeat slows, the feet and hands become ice cold, and the whole body becomes stiff like a corpse. Energy flows from all over the body towards some point. It happens differently every time. The whole process takes forty-eight or forty-nine minutes. During this time the stream of thoughts continues, but there is no reading of the thoughts. At the end of this period you "conk out." The stream of thought is cut. There is no way of knowing how long that cut lasts; it is not an experience. There is nothing you can say about that time of being conked out. That can never become part of your conscious existence or conscious thinking.

You don't know what brings you back from death. If you had any will at that moment, you could decide not to come back. When the conking out is over, the stream of thought picks up exactly where it left off. Dullness is over; clarity is back. The body feels very stiff. Slowly it begins to move of its own accord, limbering itself up. The movements are more like the Chinese T'ai Chi than like Hatha Yoga. The disciples observed the things that were happening to the teachers, probably, and embodied them and taught hundreds of postures. But they are all worthless; it is an extraordinary movement. Those who have observed my body moving say it looks like the motions of a newly born baby. This conking out gives a total renewal of the senses, glands, and nervous system. After it they function at the peak of their sensitivity.

You shall not taste of death, for there is no death for you. You cannot experience your own death. Are you born? Life and death cannot be separated. You have no chance whatsoever of knowing for yourself where one begins and the other ends. You can experience the death of another, but not your own. The only death is physical death; there is no psychological death.

Why are you so afraid of death?

Your experiencing structure cannot conceive of any event that it will not experience. It even expects to preside over its own dissolution, and so it wonders what death will feel like. It tries to project the feeling of what it will be like not to feel. But in order to anticipate a future experience, your structure needs knowledge, a similar past experience it can call upon for reference. You cannot remember what it felt like not to exist before you were born, and you cannot remember your own birth, so you have no basis for projecting your future non-existence. As long as you have known life, you have known yourself. You have been there, so, to you, you have a feeling of eternity. To justify this feeling of eternity, your structure begins to convince itself that there will be a life after death for you—heaven, reincarnation, transmigration of souls, or whatever. What is it that you think reincarnates? Where is that soul of yours? Can you taste it, touch it, show it to me? What is there inside of you that goes to heaven? What is there? There is nothing inside of you but fear.

Why do you dream? You have the feeling that there is somebody, a self, who is running the show of your perceptions, translating what is seen, heard and felt, directing the eyes, saying, "This is beautiful; that is ugly. I will look at this; I will not look at that." You cannot control like that. You think that you can, but the camera is taking pictures all the time, and the tape-recorder is recording all the time, whether you look at one thing for a longer time than you look at something else. Then, when the body is at rest or your thoughts are in a passive state, these things begin to come up—one bit of this, one bit of that. It creates some kind of a mosaic and you begin to dream. When that "somebody" is not there, there is nothing that says, "I was asleep, I was dreaming, and now I am awake."

What is morality? It is not the following of enjoined rules of conduct. It is not a question of standing above temptations, or of conquering hate, anger, greed, lust, and violence. Questioning your actions before and after creates the moral problem. What is responsible for this situation is the faculty of distinguishing between right and wrong and influencing your actions accordingly.

Life is action. Unquestioned action is morality. Questioning your actions is destroying the expression of life. A person who lets life act in its own way without the protective movement of thought has no self to defend. What need will he have to lie or cheat or pretend or to commit any other act that his society considers immoral?

What is keeping you from being in your natural state? You are constantly moving way from yourself. You want to be happy, either permanently or at least for this moment. You are dissatisfied with your everyday experiences, and so you want some new ones. You want to perfect yourself, to change yourself. You are reaching out, trying to be something other than what you are. It is this that is taking you away from yourself.

Society has put before you the ideal of a perfect man. No matter in which culture you were born, you have scriptural doctrines and traditions handed down to you to tell you how to behave. You are told that through due practice you can even eventually come into the state attained by the sages, saints, and saviors of mankind. And so you try to control your behavior, to control your thoughts, to be something unnatural.

We are all living in a "thought sphere." Your thoughts are not your own; they belong to everybody. There are only thoughts, but you create a counter-thought, the thinker, with which you read every thought. Your effort to control life has created a secondary movement of thought within you, which you call the "I." This movement of thought within you is parallel to the movement of life, but isolated from it; it can never touch life. You are a living creature, yet you lead your entire life within the realm of this isolated, parallel movement of thought. You cut yourself off from life. That is something very unnatural.

The natural state is not a thoughtless state. That is one of the greatest hoaxes perpetrated for thousands of years on poor, helpless Hindus. You will never be without thought until the body is a corpse, a very dead corpse. Being able to think is necessary to survive. But in this state, thought stops choking you; it falls into its natural rhythm. There is no longer a "you" who reads the thoughts and thinks that they are "his."

Have you ever looked at that parallel movement of thought? The books on English grammar will tell you that *I* is a first person singular pronoun, subjective case, but that is not what you want to know. Can you look at that thing you call I? It is very elusive. Look at it now, feel it, touch it, and tell me. How do you look at it? And what is the thing that is looking at what you call I? This is the crux of the whole problem. The one that is looking at what you call I is the "I." It is creating an illusory division of itself into subject and object, and through this division it is continuing. This is the divisive nature that is operating in you, in your consciousness. Continuity of its existence is all that interests it. As long as you want to understand that "you" or to change that "you" into something spiritual, into something holy, beautiful, or marvelous, that "you" will continue. If you do not want to do anything about it, it is not there, it's gone.

How do you understand this? I have for all practical purposes made a statement: "What you are looking at is not different from the one who is looking." What do you do with a statement like this? What instrument do you have at your disposal for understanding a meaningless, illogical, irrational statement? You begin to think. Through thinking, you cannot understand a thing. You are translating what I am saying, in terms of the knowledge you already have, just as you translate everything else, because you want to get something out of it. When you stop doing that, what is there is what I am describing. The absence of what you are doing—trying to understand, or trying to change yourself—is the state of being that I am describing.

Is there a beyond? Because you are not interested in the everyday things and the happenings around you, you have invented a thing called the *beyond,* or *timelessness,* or *God, Truth, Reality, Brahman, enlightenment,* or whatever, and you search for that. There may not be any beyond. You don't know a thing about that beyond. Whatever you know is what you have been told, the knowledge you have about that. So you are projecting that knowledge. What you call *beyond* is created by the knowledge you have about that beyond; and whatever knowledge you have about a beyond is exactly what you will experience. The knowledge creates the experience, and the experience then strengthens the knowledge.

What you know can never be the beyond. Whatever you experience is not the beyond. If there is any beyond, this movement of "you" is absent. The absence of this movement probably is the beyond, but the beyond can never be experienced by you. It is when the "you" is not there. Why are you trying to experience a thing that cannot be experienced?

You must always recognize what you are looking at, otherwise you are not there. The moment you translate, the "you" is there. You look at something and recognize that it is a bag, a red bag. Thought interferes with the sensation by translating. Why does thought interfere? And can you do anything about it? The moment you look at a thing, what comes inside of you is a word such as *bag.* If not *bag,* then *bench,* or *banister, step.* "That man sitting there, he has white hair." It goes on and on—you are repeating to yourself all the time. If you don't do that, you are preoccupied with something else: "I'm getting late for the office." You are either thinking about something that is totally unrelated to the way the senses are functioning at this moment, or else you are looking and saying to yourself, "That's a bag, that's a red bag," and so on and so on. That is all that is there. The word *bag* separates you from what you are looking at, thereby creating the "you." Otherwise there is no space between the two.

Every time a thought is born, you are born. When the thought is gone, you are gone. But the "you" does not let the thought go, and what gives continuity to this "you" is the thinking. Actually there is no permanent entity in you, no totality of all your thoughts and experiences. You think that there is "somebody" who is thinking your thoughts, "somebody" who is feeling your feelings. That's the illusion. I can say it is an illusion, but it is not an illusion to you.

Your emotions are more complex, but it is the same process. Why do you have to tell yourself that you are angry, that you are envious of someone else, or that sex is bothering you? I am not saying anything about fulfilling or not fulfilling. There is a sensation in you, and you say that you are depressed or unhappy or blissful, jealous, greedy, envious. This labeling brings into existence the one who is translating this sensation. What you call "I" is nothing but this word *red bag, bench, steps, banister, light bulb, angry, blissful, jealous,* or whatever. You are putting your brain cells to unnecessary activity, making the memory cells operate all the time, destroying the energy that is there. This is only wearing you out.

This labeling is necessary when you must communicate with someone else or with yourself. But you communicate with yourself all the time. Why do you do this? The only difference between you and the person who talks aloud to himself is that you don't talk aloud. The moment you do begin to talk aloud, along comes the psychiatrist. That chap, of course, is doing the same thing that you are doing, communicating to himself all the time—*bag, red bag, obsessive, compulsive, Oedipus complex, greedy, bench, banister, martini.* Then he says something is wrong with you and puts you on the couch and wants to change you, to help you.

Why can't you leave the sensations alone? Why do you translate? You do this because if you do not communicate to yourself, you are not there. The prospect of that is frightening to the "you."

Whatever you experience—peace, bliss, silence, beatitude, ecstasy, joy, God knows what—will be old, second-hand. You already have knowledge about all of these things. The fact that you are in a blissful state or in a state of tremendous silence means that you know about it. You must know a thing in order to experience it. That knowledge is nothing marvelous or metaphysical. *Bench, bag, red bag,* is the knowledge. Knowledge is something that is put into you by somebody else, and he got that from somebody else. It is not yours.

Can you experience a simple thing like that bench that is sitting across from you? No, you only experience the knowledge you have about it. And the knowledge has come from some outside agency, always. You think the thoughts of your society, feel the feelings of your society, and experience the experiences of your society. There is no new experience.

So, all that any man has ever thought or felt must go out of your system. And you are the product of all that knowledge. That's all you are.

What is thought? You don't know a thing about it. All that you know about what you call *thought* is what you have been told. How can you do anything with it—mold it, control it, shape it, or stop it? You are all the time trying to do something with it because somebody has told you that you must change this or replace that, hold on to the good thoughts and not the bad thoughts. Thoughts are thoughts; they are neither good nor bad. As long as you want to do something with whatever is there, you are thinking. Wanting and thinking are not two different things. Wanting to understand means there is a movement of thought. You are adding momentum to that movement, giving it continuity.

The senses function unnaturally in you because you want to use them to get something. Why should you get anything? Because you want what you call the "you" to continue. You are protecting that continuity. Thought is a protective mechanism. It protects the "you" at the expense of something or somebody else. Anything born out of thought is destructive. It will ultimately destroy you and your kind.

It is the repetitive mechanism of thought that is wearing you out. So, what is it that you can do about it? That's all that you can ask. That's the one and the only question, and any answer that I or anybody gives adds momentum to that movement of thought. What is it that you can do about it? Not one thing. It's too strong. It has the momentum of millions of years. You are totally helpless, and you cannot be conscious of that helplessness.

If you practice any system of mind control, automatically the "you" is there, and through this it is continuing. Have you ever meditated, really seriously meditated? Or do you know anyone who has? Nobody does. If you seriously meditate, you'll wind up in the loony bin. Nor can you practice mindfulness trying to be aware every moment of your life. You cannot be aware; you and awareness cannot co-exist. If you could be in a state of awareness for one second by the clock, once in your life, the continuity would be snapped. The illusion of the experiencing structure, the "you," would collapse, and everything would fall into the natural rhythm. In this state you do not know what you are looking at. That is awareness. If you recognize what you are looking at, you are there, again experiencing the old, what you know.

What makes one person come into his natural state, and not another person? I don't know. Perhaps it's written in the cells. It is acausal. It is not an act of volition on your part. You can't bring it about. There is absolutely nothing you can do. You can distrust any man who tells you how he got into this state. One thing you can be sure of is that he cannot possibly know himself, and cannot possibly communicate it to you. There is a built-in triggering mechanism in the body. If the experiencing structure of thought happens to let go, the other thing will take over in its own way. The functioning of the body will be a totally different functioning, without the interference of thought, except when it is necessary to communicate with somebody. To put it in the boxing-ring phrase, you have to "throw in the towel," be totally helpless. No one can help you, and you cannot help yourself.

This state is not in your interest. You are only interested in continuity. You want to continue, probably on a different level, and to function in a different dimension, but you want to continue somehow. You wouldn't touch this with a barge pole. This is going to liquidate what you call "you," all of you—higher self, lower self, soul, Atman, conscious, subconscious—all of that. You come to a point, and then you say, "I need time." So sadhana [inquiry and religious endeavor] comes into the picture, and you say to yourself, "Tomorrow I will understand." This structure is born of time and functions in time, but does not come to an end through time. If you don't understand now, you are not going to understand tomorrow. What is there to understand? Why do you want to understand what I am saying? You can't understand what I am saying. It is an exercise in futility on your part to try to relate the description of how I am functioning to the way you are functioning. This is a thing that I cannot communicate. Nor is any communication necessary. No dialogue is possible. When the "you" is not there, when the question is not there, what is, is understanding. You are finished. You'll walk out. You will never listen to anybody describing his state or ask any questions about understanding at all.

What you are looking for does not exist. You would rather tread an enchanted ground with beatific visions of a radical transformation of that non-existent self of yours into a state of being which is conjured up by some bewitching phrases. That takes you away from your natural state. It is a movement away from yourself. To be yourself requires extraordinary intelligence. You are "blessed" with that intelligence. Nobody need give it to you, nobody can take it away from you. He who lets that express itself in its own way is a natural man.

Chapter 3

No Power Outside of Man

An Interview by Professor HSK, Mysore, India, 1980

What is necessary for man is to free himself from the entire past of mankind, not only his individual past. That is to say, you have to free yourself from what every man before you has thought, felt, and experienced. Then only is it possible for you to be yourself. The whole purpose of my talking to people is to point out the uniqueness of every individual. Culture or civilization or whatever you might call it has always tried to fit us into a framework. Man is not man at all. I call him a "unique animal." And man will remain a unique animal as long as he's burdened by the culture.

Nature, in its own way, produces from time to time some flower, the end product of human evolution. This cannot be used by the evolutionary process as a model for creating another one. That is why I say this is the end product of human evolution. If it produces one flower, that's it, you see. Such a flower, you can put it in a museum and look at it. That's all you can do.

You don't like what I'm saying, because it undermines the whole Indian culture and the psychological superstructure that has been built on the Freudian fraud. That is why the psychologists and religious people are against me. They don't like what I'm saying. That is their livelihood. The whole thing is finished. The whole religious and psychological business will be finished in the next ten or twenty years.

Sir, what part has India to play in the present-day world crisis?

The crisis through which the world is passing has to produce something [in order for the world] to save itself. I think it has to come, and it will come from the West. I don't know from where, but India has no chance.

Is the questioning genuine there in the West?

It is very genuine. They are questioning their values. Now it is only at the stage of rebellion and reaction, but they want answers. They are very pragmatic people. They want answers; they are not satisfied with just promises.

So that seems to be the situation. Otherwise man is doomed, you see. But man will not disappear; he will somehow survive. I am not preaching a theory of doom. I am no prophet of doom. But I believe that it will come from the West. You see, it has to come from somewhere, and India will not be that country.

You are quite sure?

I am certain of that because half my life I've spent in the West—the first half in India, and now the second half in the West.

How do you come to this conclusion? Don't you think that India has evolved some sort of a philosophy?

Yesterday I quoted a passage from Emerson. It's very rarely I quote anybody. You see, he makes a statement, a very interesting statement, that if you want your neighbor to believe in God, let him see what God can make you like. There is no use talking about God as love, God as truth, God as this, God as that.

So, this is the most interesting thing. Let the world see what God can make you like. In exactly the same way, you have to set your house in order. India is in chaotic condition; nobody knows where it is going. So, if there is anything to your spiritual heritage (and there is a lot; I'm not for a moment denying that; India has produced so many sages, saints, and saviors of mankind), if that heritage cannot help this country to put its own house in order, how do you think this country can help the world? That is one thing.

Number two: you have to use the modern terminology, the new phrases. The people in the West are interested, fascinated, because of the new terminology, the new phrases. So they learn all these things, and they feel that they are somebody because they are able to repeat these things. That's all there is to it. You learn a new language and start speaking in that language, so you feel just great, but basically it is not in any way helping you.

So, how can this great heritage, of which all Indians are so proud, help this country first? Why is it not able to help this country? That is my question.

Help, in what sense?

First of all, you must have economic stability. Everybody must be fed, clothed, and given shelter. There is no excuse for the poverty in this country. For thirty years we have been a free country. Why do these things still continue in this country? Not that I have answers. I don't have answers. If I had the answers, I wouldn't be sitting here talking. I would do something. You see, individually, there isn't anything any-body can do. That is the situation. Collective action means trouble— my party, my system, my technique, your party, your system, your technique. So all these systems finally end up on the battlefield. All their energies are wasted in trying to win over the people to their polit-ical stands. But the problems have not in any way been solved by these systems. That's all I'm trying to say.

The country cannot save itself? The heritage cannot be of any help?

The country cannot save itself. The heritage doesn't seem to be able to come to the aid of the people, unfortunately. The psychologists, for example, have come to the end of their tether. Now they are looking to India. They are going to all these holy men, these yogis, to those who teach. They are really interested, but they want that to be put to test. They want results, you see, not just talk, not just some spiritual expe-riences and some spiritual fantasies. It must be applied to solve the problems of the world. That is all they are interested in. So, my argument or my emphasis is that they have to come out with solutions for their problems. The scientists have their problems; the technologists have their problems. They have to come out with the solutions for their problems. That is number one. There is no use in those people turning to the holy men here, you know.

They have to find answers in their own way.

In their own field—they are the ones who have to come out with their solutions for their problems. Our solutions have no answers for those problems at all—not only those problems, but your day-to-day problems also. Man is interested only in solutions, and not in looking at the problems. You say that these great sages and saints and saviors of mankind have answers for our problems. Then, why are we still asking the same questions?

So, they are not the answers. If they were the answers, the questions wouldn't be there. The fact that we are still asking the questions means that they are not the answers. So, the solutions that have been offered for our problems are not the solutions. Otherwise, why would the problems remain as problems?

So, each individual now has the responsibility, not any particular nation—India or America or Russia. You see, the individual has to find out his answers for the questions. That is why every individual is the savior of mankind—not collectively. If he can find out an answer for his question, or a solution for his problems, maybe there is some kind of hope for mankind as a whole, because we all are brought together. Whatever is happening in America is affecting us. Whatever is happening here is affecting the other nations too.

You see, the whole world is now thinking in terms of one world—at least theoretically—but nobody is ready to give up the sovereignty of his nation. That is really the crux of the problem. The European Economic Community has joined together only for economic reasons. Every nation is still asserting its sovereignty, but that is the thing that must come to an end first of all, you see.

But how can our rich heritage help to solve the material problems?

It cannot solve them, because it is false, because it doesn't operate in the lives of the people. That is why it cannot help to solve the economic problems of this country. We have talked for centuries about the oneness of life, the unity of life. How can you justify the existence of these slums? How can you justify the existence of ten crores of Harijans [i.e. one hundred million untouchables] in this country? Please, I don't have any answers. I am just pointing out the absurdity of our claims that our heritage is something extraordinary.

It means we are not translating it into action.

We are not living up to our hopes and the expectations of our great tradition or heritage, whatever we want to call it.

That doesn't mean that our heritage is false or that our values are false.

What consolation is that to us? What good is that? That's like saying, "My grandfather was a very rich man, a multimillionaire," when I don't know where my next meal will come from. What is the good of telling myself all the time that my grandfather was a multimillionaire? Likewise, India produced great saints, spiritual giants, and we don't have even one in our midst, you see. So what is the good of repeating all the time that our heritage is so tremendous and so great, or praising the greatness of our heritage? What good is that? It must help this country. So why don't you question that? There may be something wrong with the whole business. In spite of the fact that the whole culture of India is supposed to be something extraordinary, a great culture, in spite of the fact that everybody talks of spirituality, dharma, this thing or the other, India has produced only a handful of great teachers, and these teachers have not produced others like them. Show me another Ramanujacharya. Only one Ramanujacharya, only one Shankaracharya, and only one Madhavacharya, only one Buddha, only one Mahavira. They can all be counted on one's fingers.

We're not thinking in terms of these gurus, because these gurus are like the priests in the West. India has this freedom, so everybody sets up his own tiny little shop and sells his own particular wares. That is why you have so many gurus in India, just the way they have priests in the West. In the West organized religion destroyed the possibility of individual growth. They destroyed every dissent; they destroyed every possibility of individuals blossoming into spiritual teachers as in India. But luckily India had this kind of freedom, and it produced so many.

But in spite of all that, in spite of the fact that the whole atmosphere is religious, those teachers have not produced another teacher. To me the religious thing you are talking about is nothing but superstition. Celebrating all these fasts, feasts, and festivals, and going to the temple is not religion. There can't be another Buddha within the framework of Buddhism. There can't be another Ramanujacharya within the framework of that school of thought. Either they have left behind, or the followers have created, these small, tiny, little colonies. And so all those colonies are fighting all the time. They fight in the courts about whether the elephants should have a "V" mark or a "U" mark. The whole thing has degenerated and deteriorated into such a triviality nowadays.

So, "Is India able to produce an outstanding giant like those people?" is the question that everybody in this country should ask himself or herself. That is number one. Number two: Does this religion, the heritage that you are talking about, operate in the lives of the people? And the third question is: Can it be of any help to solve the economic and political problems of this country? My answer to all these questions is "No."

Don't these two things belong to two different planes?

No. Unfortunately we have divided life into material and spiritual. That is the greatest and biggest escape that we have created. You see, it's all one. You can't divide life into material and spiritual. That is where we have gone wrong. In the West they are all religious only on Sunday when they go to church, and the rest of the week they are monsters.

What do you think? What is the good of reading those books, repeating them mechanically? People are repeating, repeating, repeating, and they don't even know the meaning of what they are repeating. I listen to devotional music every morning, not that I'm interested in that or anything. Because I am here and the radio is there, I tune in. Those devotional songs—what are they? Do they know the meaning of those things they are singing? It is pornography, I am sorry to say. Really, it is pornography. I have come to the conclusion that the composers of all those stotras [verses] were sex-starved people, so they externalized it and put it on the goddess. They do not leave out even one part of the anatomy of the woman in those stotras. I am not condemning.

You can give mystical explanations for all those things. I am not interested in the mystical explanations. That's only a cover-up, a hush-hush policy on the part of those who want to put down the questioning attitude of some of the people, who want to know why these things are there.

The worship of the bull in the temple, and the worship of Siva—you know that yoni and lingam business—has come down from the original man, to whom sex was the highest kind of pleasure that he knew. Later on man experienced the bliss, the beatitude, and all that moved over. But originally, sex was the most important thing. Even the cross is a phallic symbol.

In the church they give wine and bread. What does it actually mean? You see, they have copied it from the days of the savages. When a hero died there, they ate his flesh and drank his blood, hoping that they would acquire the great traits of the hero. So, that is passed on from generation to generation.

We are carrying on, not knowing, all those silly things that are going on. I'm not blaming, you see, but what is the heritage you are talking about? Can it really solve the economic problems of this country?

The political problems and the economic problems go together. You can't separate them; they are all one. It is all one integrated unity. Why do you separate these two things? Is it possible for you to change the country without a political revolution? Not at all possible. And political revolution is not at all possible in this country, because your constitution says that change, if there is to be any change, should be within the framework of your constitution. That finishes the possibility of any rebellion against the government that is in power. So how do you expect to change that? To get elected as an MP, you have to have millions and millions of rupees. So, once you have spent millions of rupees, you have to make money there. They are not there to serve the country—not at all—so don't blame them.

I say all these social problems have to be handled by the government. There is no room for any private charity anywhere in this world. If the government does not do its duty, throw the government out. Make them do it. So, if they don't do it, you are responsible for it. Why blame the politicians? Blame yourself.

But the government that is elected represents a particular class.

Rich people, you see—"I want my five acres of land to be assured." I have none, so it doesn't matter to me. The land ceiling—nothing affects me. Even if the communists come into power, I have nothing to lose.

Not that the communists can solve the problems—nobody, no party, can solve the problems of India. Even God, if there is a God, is singularly incapable of solving the problems of India. It is not a pessimistic evaluation of the problems of India, but I don't see how it is possible. I don't see any hope for this country. I want this country to play a very important role in the affairs of the world. I would be most enchanted if India could play an important part. [laughs] Even God cannot do it. The all-powerful, almighty God—I don't know if there is any—if he can't do it, what can you and I do?

You see, the people are so weak, Sir, that they don't blow up the whole thing. If the whole thing is blown up, probably there is some chance. You see, the problem of this country is that India got her freedom handed to her on a gold platter, whereas all the other countries worked so hard and fought for their freedom, died for freedom. That's really the problem. It was a pity that the British ruled India. If the French or some others had ruled India, it would have been a different country. China had those tremendous military leaders. India cannot produce one leader like Mao Tse-Tung. How can India produce a man like Mao Tse-Tung?

But, you see, there's no point in looking to those communist nations as a model. India has to evolve its own indigenous revolution. Mao Tse-Tung would be a total failure here. So it has to produce an indigenous product (if I may use the word that way). But the times don't seem to be ripe for that kind of thing. You see, unless that kind of thing happens in India, there is no chance, there is no hope.

You see, the times do produce the individuals. India needed a man like Gandhi at that time, and he was ready. England needed a man like Churchill, and there he was. France needed a man like de Gaulle, and there was the man. Germany needed a man like Hitler, and the man was there. Not that I am supporting Hitler, but Hitler alone was not responsible. The whole nation was behind him at that time. If you blame Hitler, you have to blame every German. He was a product of the times. Immediately after the war, the English threw Churchill out. That was a great nation. England was really a great nation. They knew that Churchill wouldn't be of any help to solve the problems of England. I do not personally believe that it was because of Gandhi that India got freedom. The world conditions were such that the British had to be very friendly and walk out of India in a friendly way. You see, that was our tragedy. So, for how long this will continue, I don't know.

You see, I'm not working for India in any way, so I have no right to criticize India. Because we are sitting here, this is armchair politics we are discussing. But I have no right to say anything against anybody in India, because I am not working here.

If I find the way, I will be the first one to show you. I don't see any way. I don't believe in the revivalism of this religion, which is dead. What do you want to revive in this country? You tell me. There is nothing to revive. Build more temples? What for? There are so many thousands of temples. Why add one more temple? That means it's only for my own self-aggrandizement, not for the religious welfare of this country. Another ashram? What for? There are so many ashrams, so many gurus.

So, that seems to be the situation. We are all so helpless. We have hope. Maybe one day India will produce the right type of man, but the conditions are not ripe. When they will be ripe, I do not know. The attitude of the people is very strange in this country. The fatalism that India has practiced for centuries is responsible for the present sorry state of affairs in this country.

Do you think that the efforts of all those sages—persons like, for example, Sai Baba—are all useless?

What is he doing, Sir? What is he doing? And if he's an avatar as he claims he is, and if he can't do it, who else can? Tell me. So something is wrong somewhere.

So it is all futile?

I feel it is futile. They can't do anything.

They are doing miracles, producing something out of the void.

What good is that? What good is that—miracles? But he cannot perform the miracle of all miracles, which is necessary to transform the
whole of life, the whole way of thinking. Can he do that?

*A large number of people, including so-called intelligent people, are attract-
ed by him.*

The intelligent people are the dullest and dumbest people. [laughter]
They are the most gullible people. I am not referring to Sai Baba in particular. I don't know anything about Sai Baba. I am not interested in miracles, you see. He is the number one holy man in this country because
he draws huge audiences. So, in that respect he is number one, and there
are numbers two, three, four, you see. We have classifications according
to the number of people they draw.

So, what he can do, I don't know. I'm not interested in materializing
watches, Swiss or HMT watches. It will be the miracle of all miracles, and
if there is any avatar in this world who can perform that miracle, I'll be
the first one to salute him, that's all. He can't do it. Nobody can do it.

It's not the avatars that can help; it's the individual that can help. It is
an individual problem, so it is not the avatar who can help. There is a
savior in every individual, and if that savior is brought out, if he blos-
soms, then there is hope. But when?

*The Upanishadic seers, I think, were all people who blossomed indi-
vidually.*

U.G: Sir, if there were anything to the teachings of the Upanishads,
there wouldn't have been any need for Buddha to come. Why did he?
They created the opportunity, the need for a man like Buddha. He
came after the Upanishads. You see, the Vedic stuff deteriorated, then
the Upanishadic seers arrived on the scene. And they messed up the
whole thing, so Buddha came, and afterwards, so many people.
Buddhism deteriorated in this country, so Shankara had to come. And
Shankara's followers did exactly the same thing, so there arose the need
for Ramanujacharya to come. It's the same thing, you see—and, after
him, Madhavacharya. Where is the room for all these teachers?

So, probably there is again a need for another teacher. God alone knows. If he is there around the corner, I don't know. Even the avatars we have in our midst seem unable to perform this miracle, which is necessary to save this country and the world.

What is your concept of God? Very often you say that God alone can help.

No, that's a manner of speaking. [laughs] Man has to be saved from God; that is very essential. I don't mean God in the sense in which you use the word *God*. I mean all that *God* stands for, not only God, but all that is associated with that concept of God, even karma, reincarnation, rebirth, life after death, the whole thing, the whole business of what you call the "great heritage of India." Man has to be saved from the heritage of India. Not only the people—the country has to be saved from that heritage. (Not by revolution, not the way they have done it in the communist countries. That's not the way. I don't know why; you see, this is a very tricky subject.) Otherwise there is no hope for the individual and no hope for the country.

Not that he should become anti-God or an atheist. To me, the theist [the believer in God], the non-believer in God, and the one that comes in between and calls himself an agnostic—all of them are in the same boat.

I personally feel that there is no power outside of man. Whatever power is out there is inside man. So, if that is the case—and that is a fact to me—there is no point in externalizing that power and creating some symbol and worshipping it, you know? So that's why I say that God, the question of God, is irrelevant to man today. I don't know if I make myself clear.

It's not that you should burn all the religious books and tear down all the temples. That is too silly, too ridiculous, because what temples and religious books stand for is in the man, it is not outside. So there's no point in burning all those libraries and making a bonfire of all the religious books the way that Tamilian Ramaswamy Naicker did.

So, that's why I say God is irrelevant, because man has to rely more and more on his own resources. The heritage you are talking about has produced this man here today, all that is there in him. So, that has to express itself in a new form.

If you talk of God it has no meaning at all. Everybody becomes a believer in God or a non-believer in God and ends up fighting on the battlefield. What is the point in their reviving Islam? What is the Islam all these people are talking about? And they're quarrelling amongst themselves, the subdivisions, just the way the Indians are fighting among themselves, the small religions. So, that is why I say God is irrelevant to man in the modern context. What *God* stands for is already there in man—there is no power outside of man—and that has to express itself in its own way.

So you believe in the theory of evolution?

You see, Darwin's theory is not to be considered at all. His basic statement that acquired characteristics are not transmitted from generation to generation has proved to be wrong. Maybe there is something to evolution—maybe—but what exactly do we mean by *evolution?* You see, the simple things become complex. Man has become such a complex individual today that he has to move in the opposite direction. I don't mean that we have to advocate involution. You see, there is no question of going back and starting with the year number one. Man has to start where he stands today.

But I maintain that man has no freedom of action. I don't mean the fatalism that the Indians have practiced and still are practicing. When I say that man has no freedom of action, it is in relation to changing himself, to freeing himself from the burden of the past.

What is necessary is that the individual should free himself from the burden of the past, the great heritage you are talking about. Unless the individual frees himself from the burden of the past, he cannot come up with new solutions for the problems. So it is up to the individual. He has to free himself from the entire past, the heritage that you are talking about. That is to say he has to break away from the cumulative wisdom of the ages. Only then is it possible for him to come out with the solutions for the problems with which man is confronted today.

That is not in his hands; there is nothing that he can do to free himself from the burden of the past. It is in that sense that I say he has no freedom of action. You have freedom to come here or not to come here, to study or teach economics, or philosophy, or something else. There you have a limited freedom. But you have no freedom to control the events of the world or shape the events of the world. Nobody has that power; no nation has that power.

You know that India is helpless. Even America, the mightiest, the strongest, the richest and the most powerful nation—it has been; it is not now. Even *Time* magazine does not use those phrases any more to describe America. If even such countries as Russia and America are not able to control, much less shape, the events of the world, what can a poor country like India do? Not a chance.

So the individual is the only hope. And the individual also seems to be totally helpless because he has to free himself from the burden of the past, the entire heritage, not only of India, but of the whole world. So is it possible for man to free himself from the burden? Individually, he doesn't seem to have any freedom at all. You see, he has no freedom of action. That is the crux of the whole problem. But yet the hope is in the individual, perhaps through some luck, some strange chance.

These two statements seem to be contradictory.

That makes the God we are talking about irrelevant—God in the sense in which you use the word. There is no power outside of man. That power is unable to express itself, because of the burden of the past. When once he is freed from the burden of the past, then what is there, that extraordinary power, expresses itself. You see, in that sense there's no contradiction.

He can control events?

No, not control events—you see, he stops trying to control and shape events.

He simply sails along?

Sails along with events, you see. You and I are not called upon to save the world. Who has given us the mandate? The world has gone on for centuries. So many people have come and gone. It is going on in its own way.

So he is freed from all the problems, not only his problems, but also the problems of the world. And if that individual somehow has an impact, it is something that cannot be measured, you see.

That is the ideal state of man?

You see, the animal becomes a flower. That seems to be the purpose, if at all there is any purpose in nature—I don't know. You see, there are so many flowers there. Look at them! Each flower is unique in its own way. Nature's purpose seems to be (I cannot make any definitive statement) to create flowers like that, human flowers like that.

We have only a handful of flowers, which you can count on your fingers. Ramana Maharshi in recent times, Shri Ramakrishna, some other people. Not the claimants we have in our midst today, not the gurus. I am not talking about them. It is amazing—that man who sat there at Tiruvannamalai—his impact on the West is much more than all these gurus put together. Very strange, you understand? He has had a tremendous impact on the totality of human consciousness—that man living in one corner, you understand?

I visited an industrialist in Paris. He is not at all interested in religious matters, much less in India. He is anti-Indian. [laughs] So, I saw Ramana's photo there. "Why do you have this photo?" I asked him. He said, "I like the face. I don't know anything about him. I'm not even interested in reading his books. I like the photo, so it's there. I'm not interested in anything about him."

Maybe such an individual can help himself and help the world. Maybe.

I sometimes tease our Professor here, who is an advocate of Advaita [Shankara's monism]. You cannot go beyond Ramanuja's position [qualified non-dualism], as far as philosophy is concerned. There it stops. Monism is something that you cannot talk about. For all practical purposes it doesn't exist. That is the limit. I'm not pro-Ramanujacharya or anti-Shankara. As I see it, as a student of philosophy, you cannot go beyond that chappie Ramanujacharya. You may not agree with me. As far as the philosophical position is concerned, Ramanujacharya's position is the limit, the ultimate. The rest of it? If there is a monistic situation, that is something that cannot be talked about, and cannot be applied to change anything in this world.

Man becomes man for the first time. And that is possible only when he frees himself from the burden of the heritage we are talking about, the heritage of man as a whole. (Not East and West; there is no East and West.) Then only does he become an individual. For the first time he becomes an individual. That is the individual I am talking about.

That individual will certainly have an impact on human consciousness, because when something happens in this consciousness of man it affects the whole to a very microscopic extent maybe. So, this is a simile: when you throw a stone in a pool, it sets in motion circular waves. In exactly the same way, it is very slow, very slow. It is something that cannot be measured with anything.

So, maybe that's the only hope that man has. That's the first time such an individual becomes a man. Otherwise, he's an animal. And he has remained an animal because of his heritage, because his heritage has made it possible, from the point of view of nature, for the unfit to remain. Otherwise, nature would have rejected them a long time ago. It has become possible for the unfit to survive—not the survival of the fittest, but of those unfit to survive—and religion is responsible for that. That's my argument. You may not agree. You won't agree.

Does it mean that this ideal man...

He's not a perfect man; he's not an ideal man. He cannot be a model for others.

How do you refer to him?

He's an individual. He becomes the man, freed from all the animal traits in him. You see, animals create leaders, and the animal traits are still persisting there in man. That is why he creates a leader—the top-dog—and follows.

Is he something like a superman?

He's like a flower, Sir. This is like a flower. And each flower is unique.

His state is the natural state that you very often mention?

You become yourself. You see, the shock that your dependence on the entire heritage of mankind has been wrong, that your dependence on this culture, be it oriental or occidental, has been responsible for this situation in you—the realization that dawns on you hits you like lightning. That applies to the whole as well, because the nation is the extension of the individual, and the world is the extension of the different nations. So you are freed from the burden of the past and become, for the first time, an individual.

There is no relationship between these two flowers at all, so there is no point in comparing and contrasting the unique flowers that nature has produced from time to time. They, in their own ways, have had some impact, although the whole thing resulted in some tiny colonies fighting amongst themselves, that's all. It goes on and on and on. Who is called upon to save this world?

Couldn't you say it's a colony of flowers?

But each flower has its own fragrance. If it had not been for the heritage of man, of which we are so proud, we would have had so many flowers like this. It's not that I am interpreting or understanding nature's ways, the purpose of evolution, or any such thing. There may not be any such thing as evolution at all. If it had not been for the culture, nature would have produced many more flowers. So this has become a stumbling block to man's freeing himself in his own way. What is responsible for his difficulty is the culture.

So, what value has that flower to mankind? You can look at it, admire it, write a piece of poetry, paint it, or you can crush it and throw it away or feed your cow with it, but still it is there. It is of no use to the society at all, but it is there.

If it had not been for the culture, the world would have produced more flowers, different kinds and different varieties of flowers, not only the one rose that you are so proud of. You want to turn everything into one model. What for? Whereas nature would have produced, from time to time, different flowers, unique each in its own way, beautiful each in its own way. That possibility has been destroyed by this culture, which has a stranglehold on man, which prevents him from freeing himself from the burden of the entire past.

Sir, you attained this in your forty-ninth year?

This shock, this lightning, hitting me with the greatest force, shattered everything, blasted every cell and gland in my body. The whole chemistry seems to have changed. There's no scientific evidence or medical man to certify that, but I'm not interested in satisfying anyone's curiosity, because I am not selling this. I am not collecting followers and teaching them how to bring about this change. It's something that you cannot bring about through any volition or effort of yours; it just happens. I say it is acausal. What its purpose is, I really don't know, but it is something, you see.

A transformation has come about?

The whole chemistry of the body changes, so it begins to function in its own natural way. That means everything that is poisoned (I deliberately use that word) and contaminated by the culture is thrown out of the system. It is thrown out of your system, and then that consciousness or life (or whatever you want to call it) expresses itself and functions in a very natural way. The whole thing has to be thrown out of your system. Otherwise, if you don't believe in God, you become an atheist and you teach, preach, and proselytize atheism. But this individual is neither a theist, nor an atheist, nor an agnostic; he is what he is.

The movement that has been created by the heritage of man, which is trying to make you into something different from what you are, comes to an end, and so what you are begins to express itself, in its own way, unhindered, unhandicapped, unburdened by the past of man— mankind as a whole. So such a man is of no use to the society. Quite the opposite: he becomes a threat.

The question of being useful doesn't arise?

It doesn't at all. He doesn't think that he is chosen, chosen by some power to reform the world. He doesn't think that he is a savior or a free man or an enlightened man.

Yes, the moment he says he is the savior of mankind, he establishes a tradition.

So, the moment the followers fit him into the tradition, there arises a need for somebody else to break away from that tradition.

When Vivekananda asked Ramakrishna whether he had seen, he replied, "Yes, I have." What did he mean by that?

You have to ask him. I can't answer. I don't know what he meant by that.

Perhaps every concept has relevance in a particular framework. Now he's outside that, and all those things are irrelevant, so he doesn't care to answer.

I don't care what Ramakrishna said, or what Shankara said, or what Buddha said.

You've thrown it all out?

Don't use that word. It has gone out of my system—not that I have thrown it out or any such thing. It has just gone out of my entire system. So whatever I say stands or falls by itself. It doesn't need the support of any authority of any kind. That is why such a man is a threat to the society. He's a threat to the tradition because he's undermining the whole foundation of the heritage.

You talk of the seven hills, the seven days...

There's no significance to the seven or to the things that happened to me during the seven days. No significance at all. All that is occult stuff. There's nothing to occultism at all. There's no significance to all that.

As I very often tell my friends, I don't come to India to liberate people. I don't come to lecture to people. I come here—it's a personal thing—to avoid the harsh winter in Europe. And it's less expensive here. My talking to people is incidental—I mean it. Otherwise, I would get up on a platform. What is the point in getting up on a platform? I am not interested. I have no message to give.

Everyone can attain this natural state, but it's not in his hands?

It's not in his hands; it's not in anybody's hands. But you have one thousand per cent certainty, because it is not that it is my special privilege or that I'm specially chosen by anything. It's there in you. That's what I mean by saying there's no power outside of man. It is the same power, the same life that is functioning there in you. The culture you are talking about is pushing it down. Something is trying to express itself, and the culture is pushing it down. When once it throws the culture out, then it expresses itself in its own way.

Do those who have undergone this transformation have any common characteristics?

That question does not arise here. If I compared myself to a saint, it would be my tragedy. We don't belong to a common fraternity, a common brotherhood, or any such thing. What is it that is common to a rose, a daffodil, and a grass flower? Each one is uniquely beautiful in its own way. Each one has its own beauty. Whether you like it or not— that's a different thing.

Is uniqueness the index to this transformation?

No, this individual does not feel he is unique.

No. But for others?

Probably. You see, the expression of that is bound to be unique. When this kind of thing happens to you, you will begin to express your own uniqueness in quite a different way. How it will express itself, you do not know and I do not know.

What are your views about scientists? You said that Einstein had done a great injustice to mankind.

Don't you think that he has done the greatest harm by making the atom bomb possible?

He simply said that matter and energy are interchangeable.

Which has resulted in the atom bomb. When the question came up whether America should go ahead with the weapon or not, he said, "Yes, do it, by all means. If you don't do it, Germany will do it." If not Einstein, somebody would have done that.

So he had no choice; he had to choose between two evils.

No. If you go on choosing the lesser of the two evils, you'll end up only with evil. That is what has happened to us now.

Not that I consider him enemy number one. I also consider Freud the biggest fraud of the twentieth century because he talked of some theory that really has no basis at all. So he's the confidence trickster of the twentieth century. But it has become the slang of man today; everybody is using that. So in that sense—not that I consider all these people enemies of mankind or any such thing.

This change—you call it a "calamity"?

You see, people usually imagine that so-called enlightenment, self-realization, God-realization or what you will (I don't like to use these words) is something ecstatic, that you will be permanently happy, in a blissful state all the time. These are the images they have of those people. But when this kind of thing happens to the individual, he realizes that really there is no basis for that image. So, from the point of view of the man who imagines that that is permanent happiness, permanent bliss, it is a calamity because he is expecting something, whereas what happens is altogether unrelated to that. There's no relationship at all between the image you have of that, and what actually is the situation. So, from the point of view of the man who imagines that to be something permanent, this is a calamity. It's in that sense I use it. That's why I very often tell people, "If I could give you some glimpse of what this is all about, you wouldn't touch this with a barge pole, a ten foot pole." You would run away from this, because this is not what you want. What you want does not exist, you see.

So, the next question is: Why did all these sages talk of this as permanent bliss, or eternal life? I'm not interested in that at all. But the image you have of that has absolutely no relationship whatsoever to the actual thing that I'm talking about, the natural state. So the question whether somebody else is enlightened or not doesn't interest me, because there is no such thing as enlightenment at all.

In the light of what you have said, this question may be rather irrelevant. Have you any message?

For whom?

Anybody. Everybody.

I have no message, Sir. No message for mankind. People ask me, "Why the hell are you talking always?" When I say I can't help anyone, why the hell are you here? (I don't mean you.)

I don't want to use this "flower" business. That is the fragrance of the flower. Such an individual cannot retire into a cave or hide himself. He has to live in the midst of this world; he has no place to go to. That is the fragrance of that particular flower; you don't know what it is.

You don't know the fragrance of that flower—you have no way— that's why you are comparing it: "This smells like that flower. This looks like that flower." That's all that you are doing, you see. When you stop doing that—trying to understand what that flower is, and what that perfume is which you have never known—there is another flower, not a copy of that flower, not the rose, which you admire, nor the daffodil. "An Ode to the Daffodils," some chappie wrote. Or the rose... Why has the rose become so important? Because everybody likes them. The grass flower is more beautiful than the rose. The moment you stop trying to compare this, trying to understand and even imagine what that flower is, what its fragrance is, there is a new flower, which has no relationship whatsoever with all the flowers that we have around us.

Thank you, Sir. I'm a changed man, to what I was an hour ago.

Thank you.

Chapter 4

Betwixt Bewilderment and Understanding

Excerpts from conversations in Switzerland and India, 1972 to 1980

I've no message to give to the world. Whatever happens to me is such that you can't share it with the world. That's the reason I don't get up on a platform or give any lectures. It's not that I can't give lectures; I've lectured everywhere in the world. I've nothing to say. And I don't like to sit in one place, surrounded by people asking set questions. I never initiate any discussions; people come and sit round me. They can do what they like. If somebody asks me a question suddenly, I try to answer, emphasizing and pointing out that there is no answer to that question. So, I merely rephrase, restructure, and throw the same question back at you. It's not game playing, because I'm not interested in winning you over to my point of view. It's not a question of offering opinions. Of course I do have my opinions on everything from disease to divinity, but they're as worthless as anybody else's.

What I say you must not take literally. So much trouble has been created by people taking it all literally. You must test every word, every phrase, and see if it bears any relation to the way you are functioning. You must test it, but you are not in a position to accept it. Unfortunately this is a fact, take it or leave it. By writing it down, you will do more harm than good. You see, I am in a very difficult position. I cannot help you. Whatever I say is misleading.

Put your question simply. I can't follow a very complex structure. I have that difficulty, you see. Probably I'm a low-grade moron or something, I don't know. I can't follow conceptual thinking. You can put it in very simple words. What exactly is the question? Because the answer is there—I don't have to give the answer. What I usually do is restructure the question, rephrase it in such a way that the question appears senseless to you.

The answer latent in the question is brought to the surface?

That is all. That is why I want to understand exactly what your question is. It is not a tricky thing. I don't want to throw another question at you. But I must understand that question, and then I can phrase it in my own way and throw it back at you. And you will find out for yourself, without my telling you, that the question has no meaning at all—not that I say, "Your question is a meaningless question."

You know, this dialogue is only helpful when we come, both of us, to a point where we realize that no dialogue is possible, that no dialogue is necessary. When I say *understanding* or *seeing,* they mean something different to me. Understanding is a state of being where the question isn't there any more. There is nothing there that says, "Now I understand!" That's the basic difficulty between us. By understanding what I am saying, you are not going to get anywhere.

There is another thing I want to stress. All the questions you come out with must be your own questions. Then there is meaning in carrying on a dialogue. It has to be your question. So, do you have a question to call your own, a question that nobody else has asked before?

So many questions that people ask interest us, and we feel they are our questions.

Which they are not. This you will discover. They are not your questions at all.

The questioner has to come to an end. It is the questioner that creates the answer, and the questioner comes into being from the answer. Otherwise there is no questioner. I am not trying to play with words. You know the answer, and you want a confirmation from me, or you want some kind of light to be thrown on your problem, or you're curious. If for any of these reasons you want to carry on a dialogue with me, you are just wasting your time. You'll have to go to a scholar, a pundit, a learned man. They can throw a lot of light on such questions. That's all that I am interested in in this kind of a dialogue: to help you to formulate your own question. Try and formulate a question that you can call your own.

I have no questions here at all. I come and sit here, and it's empty, but not in the sense in which you use the word *emptiness*. Emptiness and fullness are not two different things. You cannot draw a line of demarcation between the void and the fullness. But there is nothing here—nothing—so I don't know what I'll say. I don't come prepared to say something. What you bring out of me is your own affair; this is yours, not mine. There is nothing here that I can call my own. This is your property because you have brought out the answer from me. It's not mine. I have nothing to do with the answer at all. This is not the answer. I am not giving you any answers at all.

It's like any other reflex action. You ask a question, so something comes out of it. How it is operating, I don't know. It is not a product of any thinking. Whatever comes out of me is not manufactured by thought, but something is coming out. You are throwing a ball and the ball is bouncing and you are calling that the answer. Actually, what I am doing is only restructuring the question and throwing it back at you.

The question brings out the answer?

There is no answer to the question, so the question cannot remain there any more. In that sense I have no questions of any kind except the questions I need to function in this world. I have no other questions.

Your answer is only a reflection of the question?

It is not my answer, because the question does not stay there any more. The question becomes my question, as it were. Since it has no answer, it is not waiting for any answers. The question burns itself out, and what is there is energy. You can't go on for nine or ten hours; I can. It is not sapping the energy, but adding to the energy all the time. The talking is energy itself. The talking is the expression of that energy.

Suppose I ask you about quantum mechanics, say?

There, I don't know. That's my answer, so the question in any case disappears. Whatever knowledge or information I have about quantum mechanics is there, and it comes out like an arrow, straight. Whatever is put in there comes out. But such questions as, "Does God exist?" "Is life mere chance?" "Does perfect justice rule the world?"—there are no answers to those questions, so the question burns itself out.

Who am I?

[laughs] You know very well who you are.

What do you mean?

Is "Who am I?" really your question? Not at all—you picked it up somewhere. The questioner is the trouble, not the question. If you didn't pick up this question, you would pick up another. Even after forty years you will still be asking what the meaning of life is. A living man would never ask such a question. Obviously you see no meaning in life. You are not living; you are dead. If I tell you the meaning of life, where does that leave you? What can it mean to you?

Does the questioner exist?

He doesn't exist; what exists is only the question. All questions are the same. They are mechanical repetitions of memorized questions. Whether you ask, "Who am I?" "What is the meaning of life?" "Does God exist?" or "Is there an afterlife?" all these questions spring only from memory. That is why I ask whether you have a question of your own.

You say that the question, "Who am I?" doesn't remain there when you really scrutinize it?

Because you cannot separate the question from the questioner. The question and the questioner are the same. If you accept that fact, it's a very simple thing. When the question disappears, the questioner also disappears with that. But since the questioner does not want to disappear, the question remains. The questioner wants an answer for the question. Since there is no answer to that question, the questioner remains there forever. The questioner's interest is to continue, not to get the answer.

But still there is the attention to get the answer.

The attention is the questioner; the waiting is the questioner. The waiting for an answer, the hope that there is an answer to that question, is the questioner. They're not different, you see. It has transformed itself into different tricky situations. The questioner first says he's attentive. He's very attentive because he wants the answer. He doesn't want the hints that he might not. What will he do with this answer? He is attentive, he is waiting, he is hopeful. He is all those things, and why? Because there is no answer to that question, "Who am I?" You have no way of knowing for yourself.

It is the verb that links the *who* and *I.* So, *am* links the *I* and *who* as if they are two different things. *Am,* the verb, is the continuity. When the verb is absent—if it is possible for the verb to disappear—there is no need for anything to link *who* and *I;* they are the same.

If the verb goes?

The question also goes with it. There cannot be a question without that. "Who I," you see—it is a meaningless thing. *Am* has got to be there; it creates the divisive movement there. And so you have created the question. And that question implies that there is an answer to that question; otherwise you would not put that question to yourself. All questions are there because you have a vague answer for the question: "There must be something other than what I am now," you see. I don't know if I make myself clear.

Sir, what will happen after death?

All questions about death are meaningless, especially for a young person like you. You have not even lived your life. Why do you ask that silly question? Why are you interested in that? A person who is living has no time to ask such questions. Only a person who is not living asks, "What will happen after my death?" You are not living. First live your life, and when the time comes... Let us leave it like that. I am not interested in that kind of philosophy.

Nothing will happen. There is no such thing as death at all. What do you think will die? What? This body disintegrates into its constituent elements, so nothing is lost. If you burn it, the ashes enrich the soil and aid germination. If you bury it, the worms live on it. If you throw it into the river, it becomes food for the fishes. One form of life lives on another form of life, and so gives continuity to life. So life is immortal.

But that is not going to help anybody who is caught up in the fear of death. After all, "death" is fear, the fear of something coming to an end. The "you" as you know yourself, the "you" as you experience yourself— that "you" does not want to come to an end. But it also knows that this body is going to drop dead as others do. You experience the deaths of others, so that is a frightening situation because you are not sure whether you will continue if this body goes. So then it projects an afterlife. This becomes the most important thing—to know whether there is an afterlife or not. Fear creates that, so when the fear is gone, the question of death is also gone.

You can't experience your own death. That is why I tell some of those people who are so much interested in moksha, liberation, that every one of you, all of you without exception, will attain moksha just before you die.

[laughter] But you can be sure it is too late then. The body is in a prostrate condition and can't renew itself. That death can happen to you now; it is a thing that happens now.

You have no way of knowing anything about your death, now or at the end of your so-called life. Unless knowledge, the continuity of knowledge, comes to an end, death cannot take place. You want to know something about death. You want to make that a part of your knowledge. But death is not something mysterious. The ending of that knowledge is death. What do you think will continue after death? What is there while you are living? Where is the entity there? There is nothing there—no soul—there is only this question about after death. The question has to die now to find the answer—your answer, not my answer—because the question is born out of the assumption, the belief, that there is something to continue after death.

At certain moments I am able to follow the particular chain of logic that you have expressed, and I can feel very strongly what you are saying. How that point is reached, I don't know, but once it is reached, suddenly there is great insecurity.

You see, the existence of the very thing that is questioning, the questioner, is at stake.

Yes, exactly, that produces a lot of panic.

You see, that is the trouble. You dare not question that basic thing, because that is going to destroy something there which is very precious to you: the continuity of yourself as you know yourself and as you experience yourself.

Once you dare question it, then what?

"Then what?" is absent. Then it begins to act. That is the action.

I very much want to dare. Is there a way to dare?

The question itself has the inherent capacity to find out the answer for itself. You see, if there is no answer, the question can't stay there. You are waiting for an answer either from outside or from inside. When both these areas prove to be of no use at all, what happens to that question? The rejection is not because I don't agree with the statements or experiences of others, but because they are not valid as far as I am concerned. So, it may be true, but it is not valid, so I reject them all. All outside help is finished for me. When that goes, there is no helplessness here at all. They are linked together; you really can't separate them.

The real problem is the solution. If you can't solve the problem, the problem ceases to be a problem. You are interested more in the solution than in the problem. But the solution applies only to tomorrow, not to the present—when are you going to solve the problem?—so it is not the solution. Why are you interested in finding out the solutions? They have not helped you. But you are looking at the solutions. You are interested in the solutions, not the problem. What is the problem? That is all I am asking. You have no problem there, but you are talking of solutions.

You are not satisfied with the answers given by others. You come to me. You think I am a realized man. Answers have been given to those questions, but still you put this question. You want confirmation of what you know, but this man says something that does not fit into your framework, so you don't agree with me. You have to find out the answer to that question.

The search ends with the realization that there is no such thing as enlightenment. By searching, you want to be free from the self, but whatever you are doing to free yourself from the self is the self. How can I make you understand this simple thing? There is no "how." If I tell you that, it will only add more momentum to that search, strengthen that momentum. That is the question of all questions: "How, how, how?"

The "how" will remain as long as you think that the answers given by others or by me are the answers. As long as you depend upon the answers of those people whom you think are the ones to give you the answers, the questions will remain there permanently. They are not the answers. If they were, the questions would not be there. It has to be your answer.

And the answer must be found without any process. Any process takes you away from the question, waters down the question. The question becomes more and more intense in its own way. You don't want anything except the answer to that question. Nothing else. Nothing interests you any more except the answer for that question. Day in and day out, all the rest of your life, that is the only question for you—"How?"

That "how?" is related to the answers given by others, so you have to reject all those answers. The question has to burn itself out, and the question cannot burn itself out so long as you are waiting for an answer either from within or from without. When the question burns itself out, what is there begins to express itself. It is your answer, not anybody else's answer. You don't even have to find the answer, because the answer is already there and will somehow express itself. You don't have to be a scholar, you don't have to read books, you don't have to do anything. What is there begins to express itself.

So, do you want an answer to that question that badly? You know, even those who spent their lives standing on their heads or hanging from the trees got nowhere. Anthills grew around them, and they got nowhere. It is not that simple. When this thing happened to me, I realized that all my search was in the wrong direction, and that this is not something religious, not something psychological, but a purely physiological functioning of the senses at their peak capacities. That was the answer to my question.

All questions are variations of the same question; they are not different questions. How earnest are you? How serious are you? How badly do you want the answer to that question? A question is born out of the answers that you already know. You want to know what my state is and make it part of knowledge, your knowledge, i.e. the tradition. But knowledge must come to an end. How can you understand this simple thing? Your wanting to know only adds momentum to your knowledge. It is not possible to know what this is, because knowledge is still there and is gathering momentum. The continuity of knowledge is all you are interested in.

If books could teach people anything, the world would be a paradise. Technical matters, yes—how to fix a tape-recorder and so on—but books on matters like this have no value. I don't know whether there is any value in this conversation or dialogue. But I want to make it very clear that there is no movement. You are not going to move from what you are. You haven't even taken one step. There is no need for you to take any step.

I'm convinced that in our meeting it is not the words that are important, but that there is something beyond the words.

I don't know, and you can't be sure. It may be a projection of your own. If there is anything, it acts in its own way. This consciousness that is functioning in me, in you, in the garden slug and earthworm outside, is the same. In me it has no frontiers; in you there are frontiers. You are enclosed in that. Probably this unlimited consciousness pushes you, I don't know. Not me; I have nothing to do with it. It is like the water finding its own level, that's all. That is its nature. That is what is happening in you. Life is trying to destroy the enclosing thing, that dead structure of thought and experience, which is not of its nature. It's trying to come out, to break open. You don't want that. As soon as you see some cracks there, you bring some plaster and fill them in and block it again. It doesn't have to be a so-called self-realized man or spiritual man or God-realized man that pushes you. Anything, that leaf there, teaches you just the same if only you let it do what it can. You must let that do. I have to put it that way. Although "let that do" may imply that there is some kind of volition on your part. That's not what I mean.

What is life?

You will never know what life is. Nobody can say anything about life. You can give definitions, but those definitions have no meaning. You can theorize about life, but that is a thing that is not of any value to you. It cannot help you to understand anything. So you don't ask questions like, "What is life?" you know. There is no answer to that question, so the question cannot stay there any longer. You really don't know, so the question disappears. You don't let that happen there, because you think there must be an answer. If you don't know the answer, you think there may be somebody in this world who can give an answer to that question. "What is life?" Nobody can give an answer to that question. We really don't know. So the question cannot stay there. The question burns itself out, you see. The question is born out of thought, so when it burns itself out, what is there is energy. There's a combustion. Thought burns itself out and gives physical energy. In the same way, when the question is burnt, along with it goes the questioner also. The question and the questioner are not two different things. When the question burns itself out, what is there is energy. You can't say anything about that energy. It is already manifesting itself, expressing itself in a boundless way. It has no limitations, no boundaries. It is not yours, not mine; it belongs to everybody. You are part of that. You are an expression of that. Just as the flower is an expression of life, you are another expression of life. What is behind all this is life. What it is, you will never know.

You are not different from the animal. You don't want to accept that fact. The only difference is that you think. Thinking is there in the animal also, but it has become very complex in the case of man. That's the difference. Don't tell me that animals do not think; they do think. But in man it has become a very complex structure, and the problem is how to free yourself from this structure and use it only as an instrument to function in this world. It has no other use at all. It has only a contingent value, to communicate something, to function in the workaday world. "Where is the railway station? Where can I get tomatoes? Where is the market?" That's all. Not philosophical concepts—that has no meaning at all. Wanting anything other than the basic needs—food, clothing and shelter—that is where your self-deception begins, and there is no end to your self-deception there. So all this thinking has no meaning at all. It is just wearing you out.

Thinking is unnecessary except to communicate with somebody. Why do I have to communicate with myself all the time? What for? "I am happy." "I am unhappy." "I am miserable." "That is a microphone." "This is a man." "He is something." Why are we doing it? Everybody is talking to himself. Only, when he begins to talk aloud you put him in the mental hospital. [laughter]

I think you are suggesting—and I agree with you—that it is a very tiresome thing to do. It is wearing us out, so naturally we seek methods to end it.

It is wearing you out, and all methods that we use are adding more and more to that, unfortunately. All techniques and systems are adding to that. There is nothing you can do to end thinking.

All right then, how did you do it?

"How not to think?" is your question. Do you know what that question implies? You want some way, some method, some system, some technique, and you still continue to think.

I don't want to think. If this question is wrong, perhaps you could suggest a better question.

I am not sure that you do not want to think. You see, you have to come to a point where you say to yourself, "I am fed up with this kind of thing." Nobody can push you there.

So either you can do it, or you can't do it?

You see, even then you'll find that you can't do it. You see, thought is there when there is a demand for it. When there is no demand for it you don't know whether it is there or not. I am not concerned whether it is there or not. But when there is a need for it, when there is a demand for it, it is there to guide you and to help you communicate with someone. What decides that demand is not here; it is out there. The situation demands its use; it is not self-initiated.

We are all talking of thought. Is it possible for you to look at thought? No, there is another thought that is looking. That is the tricky part, you see. It divides itself into two; otherwise you can't look at thought. When one thought looks at another thought, there are not two thoughts, but one thought. It gives you the impression that there are two thoughts, but actually there is only one movement. So, what creates the division? The division is created by thought. That is the beginning of your thinking. It is a very tricky business. It is one movement, and what is looking at what you call "thought" is all the definitions you have of thought.

"What is thought?" You pose that question to yourself. So, how can you look at that? The question is thought, you see. "What is thought?" There's no answer to that. Any answer you give is only a definition. You can say, "Thought is this." I have been saying so many things: "Thought is time; thought is space; thought is matter. Thought is this; thought is that." You know, that's all you can say.

But if you want to directly look at thought and find out for yourself, you have no way of looking at it. You have no way of finding out what thought is for yourself, because you cannot experience thought. You can experience thought only through the knowledge you have about thought. What happens when you do not accept the answers given by others? Something has got to happen to that question, "What is thought?" The question burns itself out, because it has no answer except the answer we know. That question burns itself out, and what you have in place of the question is the answer, energy. This question— thought—is matter. When thought burns itself out, what is there is energy, which is the manifestation of life. In other words, *life* and *energy* are synonymous terms.

Where does thought come from? Is it from inside, or outside? Where is the seat of human consciousness? So, for purposes of communication, or just to give a feel about it, I say there is a "thought sphere." In that thought sphere we are all functioning, and each of us probably has an "antenna," or what you call an "aerial" or something, which is the creation of the culture into which we are born. It is that that is picking up these particular thoughts.

You have no way at all of finding out for yourself the seat of human consciousness, because it is all over, and you are not separate from that consciousness. Even with all the experiments that the brain physiologists and psychologists are doing, wasting millions and millions of dollars just to find out the seat of human consciousness, they will never be able to find it out at all. I am not making a dogmatic statement or any such thing.

There is a certain capability of picking up thoughts through the antenna. Now, without knowing what exactly this antenna is, can we increase this capability?

Why do you want to increase it? I accept the limitations as a fact, you know. I am (to use your scientific term) genetically speaking limited in my capacity. I think the capacity of the individual is very limited—I don't know—genetically determined.

But even that genetic potentiality—we are using only a fraction of it.

Just a fraction. For some reason or other the culture has limited the possibility of the potential evolving into its completeness and wholeness. Somewhere along the line probably thought was necessary, but it has become the enemy of man now. It has become the enemy of man because the potential of the evolutionary process (if there is any such thing as an evolutionary process, I don't know; I can't make any definitive statement, but there seems to be something like that) is thwarted by the culture, because the culture has created a "perfect man," a "religious man," a "true gentleman," a "true blue," and so on and so on, and that is quite the opposite of what is inherent here. That inherent quality (or whatever it is you want to call it) I call *personality.*

I use the word *personality* in quite a different sense from the sense in which psychologists use the word. Every human being has a unique personality of his own, which is trying to express itself. The culture has created what is called a "normal man." You see, character building is in the interests of the continuity of the society. The character-building mechanism has suppressed and thwarted what is there inside. It is in this sense that I use the word *personality*. There is nobody like you anywhere in this world among the four billion people we have. Physiologically speaking, the individual is an extraordinary piece of creation by the evolutionary process, so I say that every individual is unique.

Whatever is there is trying to express itself and blossom into a human being. The human being has lost all of the animal instincts, and he has not developed the human instincts. What these people talk of—psychic powers, clairvoyance, clairaudience—they are all human instincts. And they are necessary because there are two things that the human organism is interested in. One is its survival at any cost. Why should it survive? I don't know; it is a foolish question to ask. That is one of the most important things. It has a survival mechanism of its own, which is quite different from the survival mechanism of the movement of thought. The second thing is to reproduce itself. It has to reproduce. These are the two fundamental characteristics of the human organism, the living organism.

The culture has made it impossible for the personality to express itself in its own way, because the culture has different ideas. It has created a neurotic state. It has created this divisive movement of thought. This divisive movement has got to come to an end if whatever is there is to express itself and come into flower. That possibility is part of the human mechanism; it is built-in there. So, this divisive movement, this neurotic condition of man, has got to come to an end. But is there anything that we can do?

How to go about it?

The problem is that anything you do—any movement in any direction, on any level—gives continuity to the structure of thought. The separation between mind and body must come to an end. Actually there is no separation. I have no objection to the word *mind*, but it is not in one particular location or area. Every cell in your system has a mind of its own, and its functioning or working is quite different from that of the other cells.

So, the whole chemistry of the body has to change. It has to undergo a sort of alchemy, if I may put it that way. Luckily, fortunately, there are certain areas in the human organism that are outside the control of thought. (This is what I have discovered for myself, you see. You can accept it, reject it, or do whatever you like.) They are the glands, what you call the "ductless glands."

Fortunately?

Fortunately and luckily, otherwise man is finished. The day you control them, that's the end of man. He will lose everything, he will become—he is already—just a nut and bolt in the social structure. What little freedom he can have, what little opportunity there is for this personality to express itself, will be lost.

These glands are outside the control of thought. The Hindus call them "chakras." The glands are located in the exact same spots where they speculated the chakras are. They are not in the psychic body. There is no such thing as a psychic body or causal body; they speculated, you see. They must have experienced what we call the "ductless glands." A tremendous amount of money is being spent, and a lot of research is going on, to find out why they are there, what the function of those glands is—the pituitary gland, the pineal gland, the thymus gland and so forth. I don't want to use the word "chakras"; I would call them "ductless glands." Unless they are activated, any chance of human beings flowering into themselves is lost. I can't say there is any such thing as an evolutionary process, but there seems to be such an evolutionary process. What its nature is, what its purpose is, I do not know, but it seems to be trying to create something. Man remains incomplete, unless the whole of this human organism blooms into something, like a flower. I don't want to use the word *flower,* because it has mystical overtones.

Actualization?

Actualization—what prevents that is the culture. The whole thing must go out of your system. Not out there—I am not suggesting book burning or tearing down the temples.

Have we the inherent power to break out of that culture?

That is you, you see. Society is there inside, not outside. That culture is part of this human consciousness, so everything that man has experienced and felt before you is part of that consciousness.

But one question for which we don't have an adequate answer is, "How is this transmitted from one generation to another generation?" It is really a mystery. All the experiences—not necessarily just your experiences during your span of thirty, forty, or fifty years, but the animal consciousness, the plant consciousness, the bird consciousness—all that is part of this consciousness. (Not that there is an entity that reincarnates—there is no entity there, so the whole business of reincarnation is absurd as far as I am concerned.) That is why in your dreams you dream as if you are flying like a bird. You see, the sex fantasies man has, the animal postures, the Kama Sutra of Vatsyayana—all that is part of that consciousness that is transmitted from generation to generation. How it is transmitted, I don't know, I can't say, I'm not competent to say. But this seems to be the means.

Much more than the genetic?

Much more than the genetic. The genetic is only part of it. Consciousness is a very powerful factor in experiencing things, but it is not possible for anybody to find out the content of the whole thing. It is too vast.

How can we facilitate the glandular functioning?

I have one thing against medical technology. You see, the very desire to understand the human being is to control him. That is why I am not quite in sympathy. The day you control the endocrine glands, you will change the personality of man; you won't need any brainwashing. Brainwashing is a very elaborate process. If nature had been allowed to go on in its own way, everybody would have become a unique flower.

Why should there be only roses in this world? What for? A grass flower or a dandelion flower has as much beauty, as much importance in the scheme of things. Why should there be only jasmine flowers, roses, or some other flower? So, the possibility is there of a change taking place which is sudden, not progressive. It has to happen in a very sudden and explosive way to break the whole thing.

In the individual?

In the individual. This has no social content at all, it has no religious content, it has no mystical content. It has none of those things. Maybe it affects the whole of human consciousness, but that is a speculation. I can't say anything about it. Anything I say is in the area of speculation. But it is bound to affect—there is only one mind, there is only one consciousness—whatever happens here is bound to affect, but its effect will be very microscopic.

How to promote this, not to control people, but to get these results?

No, the whole motivation there is to change the whole thing. The "how" you are interested in implies change. Why do you want to understand? I'm not saying you should not understand, but the motivation behind your understanding is to bring about a change. That is part of our culture. Culture demands it.

You see, there is a constant battle going on here. The battle is between what is here trying to express itself in its own way, and the culture preventing it. Is it possible, or is there any way that you can rid yourself or free yourself from the stranglehold of this culture? Can you do it through any volition of yours? You can't do a thing through volition; it has to happen. That is why I say it is acausal.

It seems to have happened to some people during the course of history. Each one has given expression to that uniqueness in his own way, and that depends upon his background. It is an expression of that background. But if this kind of thing is to happen to any individual today, it is bound to happen because nature, in its own way, produces from time to time some flower, the end product of human evolution. The end product of human evolution cannot be used by this evolutionary process as a model to create another one. If it produces one flower, that is it, you see; you can't preserve it. You can't preserve the perfume of that, because if you preserve it, it will stink. The evolutionary process or movement (whatever word you want to use) is not interested in using the one that it has perfected as a model for further creation. It has a creation of its own.

But the question you are asking is a very difficult question to answer, because it has no answer. The *how* has got to go—that is the only way. The *how* has got to go because it implies that there is a way, that there is a method, that there is a technique, that there is something you can do to bring about this total change in your chemistry, this alchemy. But any such method defeats its purpose. When you find yourself in a situation where there is no way of finding any answer to that question, that is the moment when something can happen. That is the moment when the triggering apparatus that is there helps to trigger the whole thing. The question "How?" freed from the desire to understand or bring about a change, remains there. It is a thought you see, and thought is after all a vibration. It has a built-in atomic structure. There is an atom embedded in that thought. And when that thought cannot move, when it cannot make a move in any direction, then something is going to happen to that thought.

There is only the one thought, "How?" The one question that this organism is interested in is, "How to throw off the whole thralldom, the whole strangling influence of culture?" That question is the only question this organism has—not as a word, not as a thought. The whole human organism is that one question. I don't know whether I make myself clear. That is the one question, you see, that is throbbing, pulsating in every cell, in the very marrow of your bones, trying to free itself from this stranglehold. That is the one question, the one thought. That is the savior. That question finds that it has no way of finding an answer, that it is impossible for that question to do anything, so it explodes. When it has no way to move, no space, the "explosion" takes place. That explosion is like a nuclear explosion. That breaks the continuity of thought.

Actually there is no continuity of thought, because thoughts are disconnected, disjointed things, but something is linking them up. What you call the *I* or the *self* or the *center* is illusory. I can say it is illusory, because it's the knowledge you have about the self that creates the self when you look at the self. So all the talk of self-knowledge or self-knowing has no meaning to me. It is within the framework of knowledge. It is playing tricks with itself.

So, this continuity comes to an end, and thought falls into its natural rhythm. Then it can't link up. The linking gets broken, and once it is broken it is finished. Then it is not once that thought explodes. Every time that a thought arises, it explodes. It is like a nuclear explosion, you see, and it shatters the whole body. It is not an easy thing. It is the end of the man—such a shattering thing that it will blast every cell, every nerve in your body. I went through terrible physical torture at that moment. Not that you experience the explosion; you can't experience the explosion—but its after-effects, the "fall-out," is the thing that changes the whole chemistry of your body. Then thought cannot link up any more. The constant demand for experiencing things comes to an end.

Is there somebody or something witnessing this process?

That somebody—that artificial, illusory identity—is finished. Then, you see, and even now, there is nobody who is feeling the feelings there. There is nobody who is thinking the thoughts there. There is nobody who is talking there. This is a pure and simple computer machine functioning automatically. The computer is not interested in your question, or in my question. The computer is not interested in trying to understand how this mechanism is operating, so all those questions that we have as a result of our logical and rational thinking have no validity any more. They have lost their importance.

So, the mechanism is functioning in an automatic way, but with an extraordinary intelligence. It knows what is good for it. Don't call it *divine*. There is an extraordinary, tremendous intelligence that is guiding the mechanism of the human body, and its interest is protection. Everything it does is to protect its survival. That's all it is interested in.

Then, the senses become very important factors. They begin to function at their peak capacity without the interference of thought except when there is a demand for thought. Here I must make one thing very clear. Thought is not self-initiated. It always comes into operation on demand. It depends upon the demands of the situation. There is a situation where thought is necessary, and so it is there. Otherwise, it is not there. Like that pen you are using—you can write a beautiful piece of poetry or forge a check or do something with that pen. It is there when there is a demand for it. Thought is only for the purposes of communication, otherwise it has no value at all. Then you are guided by your senses and not by your thoughts any more. So all this talk of controlling the senses is tommyrot, absolute rubbish. The senses have a built-in mechanism of control; it is not something to be acquired. This talk of yama, niyama, [controlling the senses], and all that, is rubbish. It has a self-controlling mechanism of its own. You can try to control, say, the sense of taste, but here in this state you don't have to discipline yourself or control yourself. This physical organism, or human organism, or whatever you want to call it, is guided by sensory activity alone, and not by thinking, not by mind at all.

As an ordinary human being...

I tell you, you are not an ordinary being; you are an extraordinary being. [laughter] There is no one like you. You are "the one without a second" that the Upanishads talked about.

It is not because of what you do or do not do that this kind of thing happens. That is why I use the word *acausal*—this has no cause. The structure that is interested in establishing the causal relationship is not there any more. The only thing that is left for this is survival. And the survival is limited. It has a momentum of its own, and when that is finished it is gone. This cannot reproduce another one, physiologically or otherwise. That's why I say this is the end product of human evolution. There is no need for the reproduction of another one, either as a flower or as another human being. That is why the whole chemistry of your body changes. The hormones change, and you are neither a man nor a woman any more. Such a man is of absolutely no use to this society, and he cannot create another society. [laughter]

Perfection is a foolish thought. Speaking or playing a musical instrument can be perfected, but that's not what I mean. Through years and years of practice you want to become a perfect man, but it is not something that can be perfected. There is no guarantee; there is no answer as to why this happens. This is one thing that can't be reproduced. They have placed before us the ideal of the perfect man, and that has put the whole thing on the wrong track. The perfect man doesn't exist at all. A man in whom, or for whom, mutation (if you want to use that word)

has taken place is not a perfect being. He has all the idiosyncrasies, odd-
ities, stupidities, and absurdities that are not associated with the perfect
man. It has nothing to do with that at all. He doesn't become a super-
duper genius. Tomorrow he is not going to invent something extraordinary and put man on every planet—nothing of the sort! Limitations
remain limitations—this is hereditary.

Questioning my actions before and after is over for me. The moral
question—"I should have acted this way, I should not have acted that
way, I should not have said this"—none of that is there for me. I have
no regrets, no apologies. Whatever I am doing is automatic. In a given
situation I am not capable of acting in any other way. I don't have to
rationalize, think logically—nothing—that is the one and only action
in that particular situation. Next time the action will be different. For
all practical purposes it may be a similar situation to you, but it is not
to me, because there is an unknown factor, a new factor, so my action
will be different. You may see it as inconsistency or contradiction. I
cannot act in any other way. There's no connection between the two
actions.

It is physical, not psychological. I don't remember anything that is
not happening at that particular moment. There is no reaction, only
response. But you are reacting all the time. There is the judgment for
or against: "This is right, that is wrong." The response I am talking
about is the physical response to the situation. I function in the physical plane all the time. I am not thinking of anything when I see you;
my eyes are focused on you. If I turn this side, you are wiped out. The
doorknob is there, not you. You are finished for me, even in the mind.
(There is no mind.) If necessary, it is recalled—if you ask questions.
Reaction is thinking about it: "Right, wrong, good, evil." Response is
just looking without the intervention of thought. Response is physical;
reaction is mental. You are all the time reacting. You are not physically
responding to the things out there.

If somebody tried to hit you, would you be prepared?

That is a hypothetical situation. Probably I will hit him back, I don't
know. I don't preach non-violence. Probably. I don't know, you see. The
problem is that you want to be prepared for every situation.

If somebody hit you, would you feel afraid?

There is such a thing as physical fear. That fear is essential for the protection of the human organism. It is very important. The physical organism knows what to do in a particular situation, so you don't have to think about it. There is no preparation. If there is a snake, you step back. It is finished; you don't think about it. Physiological protection is all that this physical organism is interested in, nothing else.

Life guides you. I don't want to use the word *life,* because that mystifies the whole thing. This organism is interested in protecting itself, and it knows how to survive. When I go for a walk, I tell friends, "Please, for goodness sake, look. Don't think!" You don't have to think. Just use your eyes and your ears, and they will guide you.

The vision becomes extraordinarily clear, the listening mechanism becomes extremely sensitive, that is all—not clarity of thought. Now they have what they call *sensory deprivation.* What they are trying to achieve is the opposite of this. The senses are not deprived of their activity here; they have their field day. They go where they want, think what they want, anything that comes. Like the Ganges river water— from the banks you throw half-burnt bodies, filthy sewage water, everything that is dirty. After five minutes, crystal clear. It's like that with thought. There is no good thought, no bad thought, no sensual thought, no spiritual thought. All thoughts are the same.

You may ask, "How can such a man have a sensual thought?" There is nothing he can do to suppress that thought, or to give room for that thought to act. This is a reality, a fact. Sometimes the sensual memory of making love to my wife comes suddenly from nowhere. But when these thoughts try to take root there, everything in you tightens. You don't have to do a thing. The thoughts cannot stay there. There is no continuity, no build-up. One knows what it is, and there it ends. Something else comes up. But it doesn't end there for you. You say, "How can I have these sensual thoughts?" You think you are not free if you have sensual thoughts. But if you don't have them, you can be certain that you are not a living human being. Saint or sinner, he must respond to every stimulus. There is no sublimation; all that is absolute nonsense. The saints are telling lies. It is poppycock, rubbish—don't believe all that. What is the point in condemning yourself, telling yourself that you are a sinner? What nonsense you are talking! You must respond. If there is a woman, there must be a physical response to that, otherwise you are a corpse.

But here there is no continuity, no build-up. Something else comes up. Thoughts come and go. They repeat themselves; it is fun that way. Not that I watched this as one who wanted to enjoy some fun. Most of the time you don't even know that they are there. They cannot stay there; they are moving. When you recognize there is trouble, fine, it cannot stay there for long. It is pushed out by the next thing. You don't have to do a thing. Before you realize what is happening, it is gone. When you try to look at it, it is not there. What you are looking at is completely different from what was there before. They are not problems. They become problems only when you sit in one corner trying to meditate and control your thoughts. Thoughts are welling up inside of you. How can you control it? You have no control over it. It is not possible for you to control it. All this is an exercise in futility. You don't have to do a thing.

This man is not a stone. He is affected by everything that is happening there. Nor does he bother to create an armor. The religious man has built an armor around himself. Here the cumulative process has come to an end. The only action is physical action—only on that level. The senses are running like wild horses. There is nobody who is controlling them. They run here, there, and everywhere, as the situation demands. This action is the movement of life, the real movement of life, and it has no direction. If you accept the helplessness, the problem is solved. That is why I say there is no freedom of action for you. It's not a fatalistic philosophy I am talking about, but preventing the past from interfering with, and coloring, the present.

All this talk of urdhvaretus [sublimation of sex energy] is bunkum. I make emphatic statements because it is something I have experimented with before, and I know what it is.

By conserving sex energy, you are not going to improve yourself in any way. It is too silly and too absurd. Why have they laid so much stress on that? Abstinence, continence, celibacy, is not going to help to put you in this state, in this situation. You can have sex today, and this kind of thing can happen to you tomorrow—and this can happen even through sex. If there is a moment there where there is nobody who is experiencing anything, that is the moment when this kind of a thing can happen. It doesn't have to be the discourse of a religious man. The falling of a leaf, the mooing of a cow, the neighing of a horse, or anything that is happening can do the trick, because if you don't translate anything, that will take care of it.

There is no such thing as sublimation, nothing going up there. It is only going out, but these holy men won't accept it. If they were honest enough, they would know what they are saying. So, that's what it is.

Sex is unfortunately separated from other activities. Why? I have always wondered. It is one; it can't be separated. Why have they put it on a different level? That has created the problem, not only here, but in Western countries as well. Christianity also has separated them, maybe for reasons of security or property, but now we have ways of getting rid of these things. At that time it was not so easy.

There is a beautiful term, neurotic hiatus.

Religion is responsible for that; it has created that for us. The questioning of our actions is really the moral problem. We must have new moral codes of conduct. That is necessary, otherwise we can't function. That is the trouble now. They, the West at any rate, are groping now for new codes. The old codes are all out of date, anachronistic, finished. Who cares about sex? Sex is so easy now, and everybody talks about it. One of the most epoch-making discoveries of modern times is the birth-control pill. It has changed the whole thing.

May I ask you a question? What, according to you, is a normal man? Is there one? You have, of course, divided people, and you have certain psychological or philosophical norms. Or a healthy man? What is health? I sometimes wonder who is a normal man? Not that I have a question.

What is normal is set by each society. The ordinary man wants to be with others all the time, and not alone, therefore he makes certain accommodations. That's the only definition I have.

Even such a man—the extraordinary man, as opposed to your ordinary man—has to live here in this society. He cannot run away and live in a cave and meditate. He is not in conflict with this society at all. He accepts the reality of the world, although it is so unreal, and he functions in the world, accepting the reality accepted by everybody. It is very important. I can't sit in a cave and meditate on Brahman and say to myself, "I am Brahman." This is the only reality for such a man, and there is no other reality. The ultimate reality is bosh and nonsense, it doesn't exist, it's a myth. This is the only reality. What other reality is there? As long as you are feeling the feelings of society, you are part of that society. Because you have no such thing as your own thoughts, your own experiences, or your own feelings, you can't run away from this society. You are not separate from the society; you are the society. There is no social or religious content to what I am saying.

Can I put this question back to you? What according to you is a normal man?

To me there is no such thing as a normal man. When I look at the so-called insane people, I wonder whether they are insane, or those who are treating them. I was telling a joke the other day. Some chappie in a loony bin said, "I am Jesus Christ."

His friend, another inmate, said, "I know you are not."

"How the hell do you know I am not?" said the first chappie.

The other chappie said, "I am the Eternal Father. I have created you. I should know you." [laughter] It's like that here also, when I see all those people sitting there saying "Aham Brahmasmi" [I am Brahman]. What is this nonsense?! Not that I am against anything.

You wouldn't ask that question of yourself—"Am I normal?"

No, I don't ask. Sometimes the only thing I read is *Time* magazine. I read all this stuff, you see. Why do I read it? I'm living in this world, and I would like to know what is happening in this world. Why not? All other books tell me how to improve myself, how to change myself, how to be there, how to be that. I don't want to be anything other than what I am, so I have no interest in any of those books. Some people ask why I read crime fiction. Because there is a lot of action there. If I go to see a movie, I see cowboy films. You see, there is a lot of movement there. If I watch television, I watch only the commercials.

Are you affected by what you see?

That is also affecting you in a way. You are part of this world so you are affected by that. You are not involved, but you are affected. There is a difference between getting involved and allowing yourself to be affected. All the windows are open. It doesn't matter, this or that, anything can come.

We have very strange ideas in the religious field—torture this body, sleep on nails, control, deny things—all kinds of funny things. What for? Why deny certain things? I don't know. What is the difference between a man going to a bar for a glass of beer, and a man going to a temple and repeating the name of Rama? I don't see any basic difference. Probably it is antisocial here. In the West they don't think it is antisocial. Here we think it is. These are all escapes. I am not against escapes, but whether you escape through this avenue or that avenue, an escape is an escape. You are escaping from yourself.

What you do or do not do does not matter at all. Your practice of holiness, your practice of virtue—that is socially valuable for the society, but that has nothing to do with this.

Of course we are living in society. But as far as this goes—enlightenment, realization or whatever you call it—it has nothing to do with it?

It has absolutely nothing to do with it. Why, I sometimes go to the limit of saying that it is possible for a rapist, for a murderer, for a thief, for a convict, for a con-man—this kind of thing can happen!

But has it happened?

It can happen, yes. I don't know, you see, maybe. That has nothing to do with it. The moral codes of conduct have no relationship whatsoever to this. Not that this man is immoral—he cannot be immoral. It is impossible for him, you see, impossible.

His behavior automatically conforms to the moral code prevalent in the society?

His behavior patterns probably to some extent fall within the framework of the moral and religious code. But he's a danger. What I am saying is a threat to you as you know yourself and as you experience yourself. It's a threat to you.

How?

You cannot accept this. How can you accept it?

But if it comes automatically, where is the question of your being a danger? You can't give anybody a way to achieve it.

That is the reason why I say that this individual cannot be of any use to society. He's a rare bird, a rare plant. Put him in a cage, in a museum, and look at him. He's something different, you know.

But never dangerous?

All the more, you see, because he doesn't fit into the framework.

People say that mankind's survival will be threatened even within a century.

Do you believe that? This [species] has survived for many centuries, and it is going to find some way to survive. My point is this: Not because of love, not because of universal brotherhood, not because of all that stuff, but because of the terror of liquidating ourselves, we will learn to live together. You cannot hurt anybody without hurting yourself—not psychologically, but physically. Only when we realize this, will we learn to live together. As long as each individual seeks his own security, there can be no overall security. We are talking of detente in international terms, but it has to percolate down to the level of individual relationships. Only then is it possible—not through this talk of universal brotherhood, unity of life, oneness of life. All that stuff has not helped, and is not going to help. Only terror will make us live together in peace whether we like it or not. You can take a revolver and make the world's strongest, most powerful man dance for you; it is a fact. This is going to survive somehow. You are not going to let the whole thing blow up. It's only a madcap, a lunatic, probably, who will take it into his head that it's time for all of us to go in one blow.

Man has survived for centuries, and now we are all of a sudden talking about values and all that kind of stuff. What for? It has not helped us to live in harmony and peace. We have created this moral problem, you see. Plants and animals don't have a religious problem. Man has created this religious problem.

You see, this has absolutely no social content at all, and I can't think of any collective action. So this individual is just like something produced by nature, and whether anybody recognizes him or not is of no importance. This man cannot be of any use to this society. The day they think that I am a threat to their existence, naturally they will liquidate me. I don't mind. If society liquidates me, what is left here is of no importance to me. I don't have the missionary zeal in me, or any desire to save mankind. Who has given me the mandate to save mankind? Mankind has existed for centuries, and he is going to continue. I am not in the holy business; I sing my own song. If somebody comes, I talk. If nobody comes, I go for a walk, or look at the birds, look at the trees. So many things are happening. But I don't go out and sit on a platform and talk. I am not cut out for that kind of thing. I am a simple man. I don't want to complicate things unnecessarily. You see, my position is very simple. I'm always available. I have no private life that I can call my own. Anybody can come at any time. I just see them and say, "Good morning, what can I do for you?" That's all I can do. I have nothing to give, that's all.

Knowledge is not something mysterious or mystical. You know that you are happy, and you have theories about the working of the fan, the light. This is the knowledge we are talking about. You introduce another knowledge, spiritual knowledge. But spiritual knowledge, sensual knowledge—what is the difference? We give the names to them. Fantasies about God are acceptable, but fantasies about sex are called sensual, physical. There is no difference between the two. One is socially acceptable, the other is not. You are limiting knowledge to a particular area of experience, so then it becomes sensual, and the other becomes spiritual. Everything is sensual to me.

The knowledge that is essential for the living organism—all of that is necessary. But all those speculations about God, Truth, Reality, have no meaning at all to me. They are all cultural values. They are totally unrelated to the survival of the living organism. They are all socially, arbitrarily fixed religious values. All our tastes are cultivated tastes. Likes and dislikes are all cultivated. There is no such thing as an absolute morality. By *morality* I mean questioning your actions before and after. It is all social. What is a good man good for in this world? He's good for the society, isn't he? For the smooth running of society, these codes are necessary. These religious people have created a policeman inside you. Certain actions are termed good and certain other actions are termed bad, either before or after you do them. That hasn't helped you in any way. It is thinking that has created the problem. Man's problem is basically the moral dilemma, questioning your actions before and after. It has become a neurological problem, not a religious problem. The whole of your body is involved. Even God is a neurological problem. *God* is the jumbled spelling of *dog,* but the whole of your being is reacting to the word *God.* All your beliefs—they are not just psychological; they are neurological.

You don't know what is good. You know only what is good for you. That's all you are interested in, that's a fact. Everything centers around that. All your art and reason centers around that. I am not being cynical. That's a fact. Nothing wrong with it. I'm not saying anything against it. The situations change, but it is that which is guiding you through all situations. I'm not saying it is wrong you see. If it is not so, something must be wrong with you. As long as you are operating in the field of what they call the pair of opposites, good and bad, you will always be choosy, in every situation. You cannot help doing that.

A moral man is a chicken. A moral man is a frightened man, a chicken-hearted man. That is why he practices morality and sits in judgment over others. And his righteous indignation! A truly moral man (if there is one) will never, never talk of morality or sit in judgment on the morals of others. Never!

Man is always selfish, and he will remain selfish as long as he practices selflessness as a virtue. I have nothing against selfish people. I don't want to talk about selflessness. It has no basis at all. You say, "I will be a selfless man tomorrow. Tomorrow I will be a marvelous man." But until tomorrow arrives (or the day after tomorrow, or the next life) you will remain selfish. What do you mean by selflessness? You tell everybody to be selfless. What is the point? I have never said to anybody, "Don't be selfish." Be selfish, stay selfish! That is my message. Wanting enlightenment is selfishness. The rich man's distributing charity is also selfishness. He will be remembered as a generous man. You will put up a statue of him.

The basic pleasures you are indulging in, I am not against at all. Whatever you do, I am not against it at all. Because you think there is something more interesting than what you are doing, there is restlessness. Because you have an ideal way of doing things, a perfect way of doing things. Why is this going on?

We want to feel that we have spent our life usefully.

And at the end of your life you will tell yourself that you have wasted all your life. You are not doing anything to change. You have invented a next life. Your dissatisfaction is very artificial. If you were really interested in mankind, you would really be doing something to change.

Once the question "How to live?" is dropped, living itself becomes the most important thing. You must be free from the burden of culture. Of course you can't just throw away the culture. For example, taking a morning bath and all that. But it's so simple—I also take my bath— what is so religious about it? You think that there is something more interesting than what you are doing. If that is knocked off, what you are doing becomes very, very interesting.

You have been told that you should practice desirelessness. You have practiced desirelessness for thirty or forty years, but still desires are there. So something must be wrong somewhere. Nothing can be wrong with desire. Something must be wrong with the one who has told you to practice desirelessness. This [desire] is a reality; that [desirelessness] is false. It is falsifying you. Desire is there. Desire as such can't be wrong, can't be false, because it is there. Anger as such can't be false, because anger is there. You are talking of some energy which those people have defined as God or God knows what. Don't you see that it is the very thinking that has turned this into a problem? Anger is energy, desire is energy. All the energy you want is already in operation there. What the hell do you want energy for? You are destroying this energy through thinking. It is only thinking that has created the problem. Without thinking, there is no problem there. What I'm saying is that through thinking you cannot solve the problem. Thinking can only create problems.

You hope that you will be able to resolve the problem of desire through thinking, because of that model of a saint whom you think has controlled or eliminated desire. If that man has no desire as you imagine, he is a corpse. Don't believe that man at all! Such a man builds some organization, and lives in luxury, which you pay for. You are maintaining him. He is doing it for his livelihood. There is always a fool in the world who falls for him. Once in a while he allows you to prostrate before him. You will be surprised if you live with him. You will get the shock of your life if you see him there. That is why they are all aloof—because they are afraid you will catch them some time or other. The rich man is always afraid that you will touch him for money. So too the religious man—he never, never comes in contact with you. Seeing him is far more difficult than seeing the president of your country. That is a lot easier than seeing a holy man. He is not what he says he is, not what he claims he is.

But those men who have made it—they live amongst the people. You can see them always there.

What is the meaning, the purpose, of life?

You are asking me, "Has anything any purpose?" Look here, a lot of meanings and purposes have been given to you. Why are you still looking for the meaning of life, the purpose of life? Everybody has talked of the meaning of life and the purpose of life—everybody. Answers have been given by the saviors, saints, and sages of mankind. You have thousands of them in India, and yet today you are still asking the same question, "Has life any purpose or meaning?" Either you are not satisfied or you are not really interested in finding out for yourself. I submit that you are not really interested, because it's a frightening thing. It's a very frightening thing. Is there any such thing as truth? Have you ever asked that question for yourself? Has anybody told the truth?

There are so many truths.

They are all liars, fops, fakes, and cheaters in the world, who claim they have searched for and told the truth! All right, you want to find out for yourself what this truth is. Can you find out? Can you capture the truth and hold it and say, "This is truth"? Whether you accept or reject, it's the same. It depends on your personal prejudices and predilections. So if you want to discover the truth for yourself, whatever it is, you are not in a position to either accept or reject. You assume that there is such a thing as truth. You assume that there is such a thing as reality (ultimate or otherwise). It is that assumption that is creating the problem, the suffering, for you.

Look here, I want to experience God, Truth, Reality or what you will, so I must understand the nature of the experiencing structure inside of me before I deal with all that. I must look at the instrument I am using. You are trying to capture something that cannot be captured in terms of your experiencing structure, so this experiencing structure must not be there in order that the other thing may come in. What that is, you will never know. You will never know the truth, because it's a movement. It's a movement! You cannot capture it, you cannot contain it, you cannot express it. It's not a logically ascertained premise that we are interested in. So, it has to be your discovery. What good is my experience? We have thousands and thousands of experiences recorded. They haven't helped you. It's the hope that keeps you going. "If I follow this for another ten years, fifteen years, maybe one of these days I will..." Because hope is the structure.

So he spends a lifetime and finally discovers that he's discovered nothing.

Nothing. That's the discovery. So-called self-realization is the discovery for yourself and by yourself that there is no self to discover. That will be a very shocking thing. "Why the hell have I wasted all my life?" It's a shocking thing because it's going to destroy every nerve, every cell, even the cells in the marrow of your bones. I tell you, it's not going to be an easy thing. It's not going to be handed over to you on a gold platter. You have to become completely disillusioned, and then the truth begins to express itself in its own way. I have discovered that it is useless to try to discover the truth. The search for truth is, I have discovered, absurd, because it's a thing that you cannot capture, contain, or give expression to.

Can you describe and communicate your state?
You see, the moment I try to communicate something, it is gone. It is only a shadow of it; that's not it.

Is it an incommunicable experience?

No, it cannot be experienced. You cannot communicate what you cannot experience. I don't want to use those words, because *inexpressible* and *incommunicable* imply that there is something that cannot be communicated, that cannot be expressed. I don't know. There is nothing there. I don't want to say there is nothing there, because you will catch me. You will call it emptiness, void, and all that sort of thing. [laughter]

I can only put it this way: Whatever is there cannot be experienced. Whether there is anything there, I don't know. I have no way of knowing it at all. To put it in your own Vedantic terminology, there is no such thing as the unknown at all. Whatever you know of what is called the unknown is not the unknown. Whether there is any such thing as the unknown, I really don't know. Whatever you know of that unknown, whatever you experience of what you call the unknown, is not the unknown, because it has become part of your knowledge.

What do you want? Tell me, what is it? Look here, you can't ask for a thing that you don't know, and you don't know a thing about this, now or then. Even assuming for a moment that you are an enlightened man, you have no way of knowing anything about it. This can never become a part of your knowledge.

This has understood that it is not possible to experience anything any more. I don't know if I quite make myself clear. The individuality, the isolation, the separation (or whatever you want to call it) is not there any more. What separates you, what isolates you, is your thought. It creates the frontiers; it creates the boundaries. And once the boundaries are not there, it is boundless, limitless. Not that you can experience that boundlessness and limitlessness of your consciousness—the content of your consciousness is so immense that you can't say anything about it. That is why I use the words, "It's a state of not knowing." You really don't know. But how do you know that you do not know? It's not that you say to yourself that you do not know, but in relation to the ordinary state of consciousness you have no way of knowing that at all. Nobody has any way. There is not even an attempt on your part to grasp something.

You don't accumulate experiences. If you want to experience one thing, the whole series of mysteries are there knocking on your door. That is not an experience at all. You are interested in experiencing the ultimate reality, Truth, God, God knows what. But it's futile for you to attempt to experience a thing that you cannot experience. It doesn't mean that it is beyond the experiencing structure. "It's a thing that I cannot describe, that I cannot..." You see, it's not all that stuff. The experiencing structure comes to an end. If you don't recognize what you are looking at—that flower as a flower, that rose as a rose—it means you are not there. What are you? You are nothing but a bundle of all these experiences, the knowledge you have about them.

I see, and I don't know what I'm looking at. My sensory perceptions are at their peak capacity, but still there is nothing inside of me that says, "That is green. That is brown. You have white hair. You wear glasses..." The knowledge I have about things is in the background; it is not operating. So, "Am I awake? Am I asleep?" I have no way of knowing it for myself. That is why I say that in this consciousness there is a total absence of any division into wakeful, dreaming, and deep-sleep states. This may be called turiya (to use your Sanskrit term)—not transcending these things, a total absence of this division.

There are no dreams in your world?

In a way, the whole of life is like a great big dream. I am looking at you, but I really don't know anything about you. This is a dream, a dream world. There is no reality to it at all. When the experiencing structure is not manipulating consciousness (or whatever you want to call it), then the whole of life is a great big dream, from the experiential point of view—not from this point of view here, but from your point of view. You see, you give reality to things—not only to objects, but also to feelings and experiences—and think that they are real. When you don't translate them in terms of your accumulated knowledge, they are not things. You really don't know what they are.

So, this state of not knowing is like living in a dream?

To you. In relation to the reality you give to things, you would call this state of not knowing a dream. I really don't even know whether I am alive or dead.

Here there is no such thing as reality any more, let alone the ultimate reality. I function in the world as if I accept the reality of everything the way you accept it. For example (I always ask this), is it possible for you to experience the three-dimensional space in which you are functioning? No. You must have knowledge—length so many feet, width, height so many feet. How can you experience the three-dimensional space except through knowledge? So even this cannot be experienced, let alone the fourth dimension. We really don't know about it. So I can say that the walls don't exist for me, in the sense that there is no direct experience of the wall over there. That does not mean that I will knock myself against the wall when I move in that direction. It's like the water flowing. When there is an obstacle to the water, there is an action there. Either it overflows or it takes a diversion. And that action is possible only when the knowledge that is there in the background comes into operation. Then there is an action there. But here and now, when I begin to walk in that direction, there is no question of an obstruction or anything there.

You see, if I use the word *matter*, it is not in the sense in which the scientists use the word. [touches the carpet] There is a contact. A clever man asks, "How do you know there is a contact?" That contact is awareness, you can say. But the moment you say that it is hard, you have given solidity to it. Otherwise, is it hard or is it soft? Can you experience directly? I don't know. Language is the most misleading thing. If I use the word *directly*, you think there is a direct way of experiencing something. So when I use the word *directly*, I mean that you cannot experience anything at all. When I talk of vista vision, it is not that I can experience that vista vision. What I am saying is that you cannot. Don't try to experience what I am talking about. I can't experience, you can't experience, nobody can experience. Then, why talk about it? Because you are there and I am here.

Unless you have to catch a train or something, you are living in the present moment?

To call it "living from moment to moment" is very misleading. That moment-to-moment living can never be captured by you. That can never become part of your conscious existence, much less your conscious thinking.

Look here, there is no present to the structure of the *you*. All that is there is the past, which is trying to project itself into the future. You can think about past, present, and future, but there is no future, there is no present. There is only the past. Your future is only a projection of the past. If there is a present, that present can never be experienced by you, because you experience only your knowledge about the present, and that knowledge is the past. So what is the point in trying to experience that moment that you call *now?* The now can never be experienced by you. Whatever you experience is not the now. So the now is a thing that can never become part of your conscious existence, and that you cannot give expression to. The now does not exist, as far as you are concerned, except as a concept. I don't talk about the now.

How can you expect to experience a thing that is beyond, if you can't experience a simple thing like that bench there, which you have handled and used all your life? Even a simple thing like that bench, you can't experience. What you experience is only the knowledge you have about it, and the knowledge has come from some outside agency always. It is somebody else's; it is not yours. If you experience somebody else's experience, it is not yours. Somebody else will come along and take it away. A more persuasive man comes along and says, "That's not the way to experience; there's another way," and so on and so on.

As I see it, there is no preparation for it, no sadhana, no meditation. You can stand on your head for forty years; nothing is going to happen. Probably you will experience what you can experience, anything you want. Thought is something extraordinary. You can create something—a solid object—and put it out there, touch it, feel it, experience it and talk to it. You think it is something extraordinary. You have to go through all these experiences.

Sometimes, out of nowhere, something like an experience too extraordinary to have happened to you or anybody ever before is there. But that did not come out of nowhere. It is part of the knowledge of consciousness. All that man has experienced before you is part of consciousness. It is all there. All that is a contamination. Anything you experience, however profound it may be, is a contamination. It has nothing to do with this state. Somebody has experienced that before. Anything you experience there is a worthless thing; it is not that.

Whatever is experienced is thought-induced. Without knowledge, you can't experience. And experience strengthens the knowledge. It is a vicious circle—the dog chasing its own tail.

Expansion of consciousness is nothing, but you give so much importance to that. Drugs will make it a lot easier than all these meditations and yogas. I know lots of people who have taken LSD. (Please don't misunderstand me—I am not advocating it.) You are in the presence of a huge mountain. Suddenly the consciousness expands to the size of the mountain, literally. There is a sudden blow-up of consciousness, and this sudden expansion releases tremendous energy there inside of you. What is the effect of that on the physical body? The physical body responds to what you call the sudden expansion of consciousness. The only way the physical body can respond to that sudden expansion of consciousness is by taking a sudden breath. Suddenly you take a breath, and the whole breathing pattern changes. So that is why you have that expression, "a breath-taking view." I went to the Elephanta caves [near Bombay]. They have this trimurti [religious sculpture] there—a huge thing, you know—and I was standing before it. Suddenly there was an expansion of my consciousness (or whatever you want to call it) to the size of that. You experience such things all the time. There is nothing to these experiences.

None of these experiences means anything, whether you are "this side" or "that side." Actually there is no this side or that side, because there is no line of demarcation here. The realization dawns on you that those experiences, however profound they may be, aren't worth anything, that's all. You may be in a blissful state—even after that "calamity" you have blissful states, ecstatic states, a sudden melting away of everything that is there. It doesn't mean anything. You experience, I experience. What is the difference? In India holy people experience some petty little thing called a blissful state or the absence of body consciousness and they think something marvelous is happening. All those things are limitations. They are limiting consciousness; they are not in any way helping. But to you probably they are of great interest, because man is functioning all the time in that limited consciousness.

You start with the assumption that LSD is something terrible. Why, I wonder? I'm not supporting or recommending it. Drugs only produce experiences, and what I am talking about is not an experience. But all the young people in the West have tried it—little girls and boys, everybody. That is why they are suddenly interested in this kind of stuff—the Indian stuff—not because they are dissatisfied with their wealth or their values. They have tried LSD, and it has given them some kind of feeling that there must be something more to consciousness. But they are ordinary experiences.

All those religious experiences are no different from the experiences people have when they take drugs. I know a boy who had never heard of the Tibetan literature, but when he was on a trip (as they put it), he experienced all kinds of mandalas [mystical designs]. He started talking about them, and he met one Tibetan chap who described them to him. How is that kind of thing possible? You don't have to be in Tibet. No matter where you are, you see, all that is part of consciousness. Even Donald Duck has become part of the human consciousness.

You cannot experience anything that you can call your own. Whatever you experience, however profound that experience may be, is the result of the knowledge that is part of your consciousness. Somebody must have, somewhere along the line, experienced the bliss, beatitude—call it ecstasy, call it by whatever name you like—but somebody somewhere along the line, not necessarily you, must have experienced that, and that experience is part of your consciousness. You have to come to a point where there is no such thing as a new experience at all. Somebody has experienced it before, so it is not yours.

The saint or mystic is a second-hand man who experiences what the sages have talked about, so he is still in the field of duality, whereas the sages or seers are functioning in the undivided state of consciousness. The mystic experience is an extraordinary one because it is not an intellectual experience. It helps them to look at things differently, to feel differently, to experience things differently, and to interpret the statements of the sages and seers for others.

The world should be grateful to the saints rather than to the sages. Had it not been for the saints, the sages would have been clean forgotten long ago. The sages don't depend upon any authority; what they say *is* the authority. This the sages talked about, and the saints—some of them—had experiences, and this became a part of their experience. They tried to share that experience through music and all kinds of things. But this is not an experience that can be shared with somebody else; this is not an experience at all.

The saints are trying to tell you, so they are always in the field of duality. Whereas the sage or seer, or whatever you want to call him, is in the state of undivided consciousness. He does not know that he is a free man, so for him there is no question of trying to free others. He is just there, he talks about it, and then he goes. Gaudapada had no disciples; he refused to teach anybody. Ramana Maharshi at least was our contemporary. We know something about him. He taught nobody, initiated nobody. Such a man does not depend upon the authority of anybody. Great teachers never use any authority, and they do not interpret the saints. The saints help you to look at things differently, to interpret things differently.

You cannot become a sage through any sadhana [spiritual practice]; it is not in your hands. A sage cannot have a disciple. A sage cannot have a follower, because it is not an experience that can be shared. (Even an ordinary experience, you can't share with others. Can you tell somebody who has never experienced sex what the sex experience is like?) The sages and seers are original and unique because they have freed themselves from the entire past. (Even the mystic experience is part of the past.) Not that the past goes for such a man, but for him the past has no emotional content. It is not continually operative, coloring the actions.

This is the ultimate; you have to totally surrender yourself. There is no jnana marga [path of wisdom]. There is no marga [path] at all. It is total surrender—throwing in the towel, throwing in the sponge—and what comes out of that is jnana [wisdom]. It is not surrender in the ordinary sense of the word. It means there isn't anything you can do. That is total surrender, total helplessness. It can't be brought about through any effort or volition of yours. If you want to surrender to something, it's only to get something. That's why I use the words "a state of total surrender." It's a state of surrender where all effort has come to an end, where all movement in the direction of getting something has come to an end. All wanting, be it this wanting or that wanting, is totally absent.

But, first of all, there's no hunger. A hungry man will do anything and everything to satisfy his hunger, and then he will discover that there is nothing he can do to satisfy it. Even the hope must go that some miracle will happen and it will descend upon you from somewhere. If there is nothing you can do to satisfy your hunger, something will happen. All those to whom this kind of thing has happened have really worked hard, touched rock bottom, staked everything. It does not come easily. It is not handed over to you on a gold platter by somebody.

It is a very simple thing—so simple that the complex structure does not want to leave it alone. But at the same time I ask, "Is there anything that you can do?" Nobody can create the hunger. I always give the simile of the rice husk: when once it is lighted, it goes on burning, burning, burning, until the whole thing is burnt up. It is a thing that you cannot artificially create. You will probably be inspired or hypnotized by some kind of go-getter or hypnotist. There are so many.

There is no such thing as experience here. You seem to know. You imagine. Imagination must come to an end. I don't know how to put it. The absence of imagination, the absence of will, the absence of effort, the absence of all movement in any direction, on any level, in any dimension—that is the thing. That is a thing that cannot be experienced at all. It is not an experience. You are interested in experiencing bliss, beatitude, love, God knows what, but that is a worthless thing. If I experience bliss, is that bliss? It is created by the knowledge I have. It is the knowledge. To be free from knowledge is not an easy thing. You are that knowledge—not only the knowledge that you have acquired in this life, but the knowledge of millions and millions of years, everybody's experiences. People have some experiences, you see, and on that they build a tremendous superstructure.

You say it's a simple thing, but then you say it's a difficult thing.

No, you see, the thing is so simple that the complex structure does not want to leave it alone.

I don't like the articles written about me. You are trying to present me as a religious man, which I am not. You are failing to comprehend the most important thing that I am emphasizing. These articles don't give any idea of what I am expressing. There is no religious content, no mystical overtones at all, in what I am saying. Man has to be saved from the saviors of mankind! The religious people—they kidded themselves and fooled the whole of mankind. Throw them out! That is courage itself.

What is the good of repeating "Abhayam vai Brahman" [the ultimate reality is fearlessness]? Fearlessness is not freedom from all the phobias. The phobias are essential for the survival of the organism. You must have the fear of heights and the fear of depths. If that is not there, there is a danger of your falling. But you do not want to teach courage to man to fight on the battlefield. Why do you want to teach him courage? To kill others and get killed himself—that is your culture.

Crossing the Atlantic in a balloon or the Pacific on a raft—anybody can do that—that is not courage. Fearlessness is not a silly thing like that.

Courage is to brush aside everything that man has experienced and felt before you. You are the only one, greater than all those things. Everything is finished. The whole tradition is finished, however sacred and holy it may be. Then only can you be yourself; that is individuality. For the first time you become an individual. As long as you depend upon somebody, some authority, you are not an individual. Individual uniqueness cannot express itself as long as there is dependence. You don't have to depend upon any authority; it has an authority of its own. You will never interpret anything, you will never rely on any authority, and yet you won't call yourself unique.

The problem is that even if such a person doesn't talk, his very presence becomes a model for somebody. The fact that somebody sits here from morning till evening—what can I do about it? Sometimes they go into trances. They say, "How can you deny what is happening to me?" I say, "You may do what you like." How can I convince you that I have nothing more than you have? I don't have anything that you don't have. Your wanting something from somebody is the cause of your misery. The end of illusion is the end of you. So you can't be without illusion. You can only replace one illusion with another illusion.

It is very difficult to make you understand the absurdity of the whole of sadhana. (I am blocking every escape, as it were. Even that outlet has to be blocked to put you in a corner. You must be choked to death, as it were.) Only a real teacher can find that out and tell you—nobody else. (Not those people who interpret the texts and Puranas. All that is totally unrelated.) Only such a man can talk. And such a man never encourages any kind of sadhana, because he knows that if this kind of thing has to happen to somebody, that person will not need the help of anybody. In spite of everything it will happen.

Whatever you are doing is blocking its happening. It is misleading to put it that way, because there is nothing to happen. You don't realize that whatever you are doing is a self-centered activity. Whatever you are doing in any direction is only strengthening or distorting the whole thing. The whole of sadhana is self-centered activity. It is very difficult to understand that. The instrument that you are using is born in the field of cause and effect. It cannot conceive of anything happening without cause and effect. That is why that is not the instrument to understand this, and there is no other instrument.

This is acausal. It is a quantum jump. It jumps from here to there; you cannot link up these things. You put me on the other side of the river. You want to cross in a boat. That boat is a leaky boat, and you will sink. There is no other bank, and there is no river to cross, no boat. It is very difficult for you to understand that. You have created an image and put the image on the other side. I say, "No, for goodness sake, I am on the same bank. There is no river to cross, and no boatman is necessary!"

Nobody can guide you. You have no guidelines, because he himself doesn't know. If I knew, I would guide you along. Such a man cannot guide or lead you anywhere. It is not that I am against gurus—not at all. He knows—even your books say it—that it is not the guru that can help you. It doesn't mean some sort of mysterious thing. The hymns say, "Whomever it chooses, to him it happens." That does not mean that there is any power outside of you. That potential is there in you already; it has the capacity to explode. If through some strange chance, if through some luck, thought remains by itself without splitting itself into two, something has to happen to that. It is like an atomic explosion—not one, but trillions. When it explodes, it blasts everything that is there. It is a chain reaction. One after the other, every cell is involved.

It is not so easy—not through logic or power or somebody's teaching or repeating some mantras [mystical syllables]. You cannot make it happen. But the possibility of that kind of thing happening is there in everybody because that is its nature. That is the reason why it happens to one in a billion. If you ask the question of why it should happen to that individual and not to you, it means you haven't got a chance. That has no cause—it is acausal—because I can't give you or tell you how this happened. There is no "how." That is the reason I say it has no cause and cannot be reproduced. Reproducing a copy has no value at all; that is why it cannot be reproduced. No teacher has reproduced another teacher like himself. It is not my opinion. Buddha has not left another Buddha. No teacher has reproduced another teacher like himself. While he may have followers, he has something that cannot be reproduced, because Nature does not use anything as a model to reproduce another.

All that you are doing to purify yourself has no meaning at all, because that purificatory talk is not going to help you at all. It can make you into a saint, but it cannot touch the other thing. This kind of thing can take place only in the degenerated species (so the biologists say). It is going to throw out something unique, which has not been reproduced before. It is a biological freak. So all your morality, and all your practicing this, that, and the other, has no meaning. That is why the Upanishadic seers never talked of morality or sadhana, whereas the saints have emphasized them because they are second-class imitators. This kind of thing, if it has to happen, will happen in spite of those things. And I maintain that it is genetically fixed. Only in such a man does this kind of thing happen.

Do you mean that it is unnecessary for anyone to aspire?

The aspiration is part of your consciousness. That has to come to an end. There is nothing that you can do to stop it. In other words, you cannot but do sadhana; you are doomed that way. Even if you drop sadhana, it creates a struggle in you. You will replace it with another kind of sadhana, like JK's gimmick, choiceless awareness. You begin to practice those gimmicks, the same old nonsense. The words are different, but the game is the same. But somewhere along the line the realization that that is not the thing has to dawn upon you. Otherwise you will continue listening, hoping that listening to him the next time will make you understand. There is no chance of this. If anything has to happen, it has to happen here and now.

You see, the trouble is that the more beliefs you have, the more difficult it becomes for you, because one more thing is added to your tradition. Your tradition, which you want to preserve, has been strengthened and fortified by the appearance of a new man, because you are trying to fit him into the framework of your tradition. This structure of belief is interested in protecting the tradition. But this new man is interested in breaking the cumulative nature of the tradition— not in maintaining the tradition, but in breaking it. A certain person breaks it, and you make it a part of that accumulated wisdom. That is why it becomes more difficult. Even the revolutionary statement of that particular individual who has achieved this breakthrough has already become part of your tradition. Your very listening has destroyed the revolutionary nature of this breakthrough and has made this a part of knowledge, tradition, because you are the tradition. The listening mechanism that is operating there in you is the tradition. It strengthens itself, fortifies itself, through the listening process. That is why I say that what is coming out of my mouth is no different from the barking of dogs, the howling of jackals, or the noise of cats.

By the time this has been accepted—what is coming out of me—the need has been created for somebody else to come and blast it. That is why I am talking. The very expression of this has created the need for something new to happen. That is its nature. That is the purpose (if there is any purpose)—not to create a following, but to create something new there. Something new is saving you from the burden of the past. The moment it is given expression to, it is old.

Why be like this man? Handing over the torch from one person to another and maintaining the hierarchical structure—what for? Following another is an animal quality. Man cannot become man so long as he follows somebody. What is responsible for man remaining an animal is that culture—the top dog, following somebody—that has not helped you at all. You want to be a cheap imitation of Shankara or Buddha; you don't want to be yourself. What for? I tell you, you are far more unique and extraordinary than all those saints and saviors of mankind put together. Why do you want to be a cheap imitation of that fellow? That is one of the myths. Forget it. Shankara has been dead for centuries. You have that potential. The first thing is to drop Shankara. Of course, if you are using Shankara's teachings as a means to earn your livelihood, that is another thing.

Now supposing you are "there" (let us put it that way), you will not say to yourself or to others that you are a free man, you will not try to free anybody. It is just there, like the flower. (I don't want to use that word; it has some mystical overtones.) The flower on the dung heap has a beauty of its own. The other flowers are no match for that. It will go one day. It doesn't matter.

There is nothing that you can do. That statement has no meaning for you, because you are doing something all the time. You have to do something or the other, so this statement has no meaning, no relevance to you at all. The description of this state is a very dangerous thing because you are trying to relate this to the way you are functioning. What for? Because you want to change that, improve it, modify it, or do something there in relation to what I am saying. What do you want to change there? What is it? Can you find it? Can you locate it? Can you pinpoint it and say, "This is the thing that I want to be transformed or changed. Here is where I want to bring about a mutation?" How? What is that? Can you see it? Can you locate it? Can you find it out? You cannot.

Whatever you want, you can get. Whatever experience you want, you can experience. If you don't know, there is always somebody to help you somewhere. You have to find out. Anything you want, you can experience. But whatever you experience is worthless. It is not it, because this is a thing that cannot be experienced. It is not an experience.

Enlightenment (if there is any such thing as enlightenment) is not an experience at all. So, this dawns on you—this realization (if you want to put it that way) that there is nothing to realize. Self-knowledge or self-realization is to realize for yourself and by yourself that there is no self to realize. That is going to be a shattering blow.

To whom?

The one who is pursuing. That is why it happens to one in a million, one in a billion—not because of what he does or does not do. All your doing is the barrier.

Unless you are "there," you can't understand the meaninglessness of this search at all. When you are there, you see that the very search is the self, the very thing you want to be free from. There is no "you" independent of the search (i.e. your sadhana to attain a goal). That you don't understand. It is the goal that you have set before yourself that has created the "you." If the goal goes, if you brush aside the goal, you replace one with another. You can't be without illusion. You replace one illusion with another. If illusion goes, you go.

If you accept the goal, it is all right with me, but I say that the goal itself is false. You say that is what you want to achieve, so all this sadhana is necessary. I maintain that there is nothing to be achieved, nothing to be accomplished, nothing to be attained, so all that you are doing to achieve your goal is meaningless. I didn't understand that when I was doing all that sadhana. The earlier it dawns on you, the better for you. If those things produce some experiences, it will be very difficult for you to transcend your own experience. Somewhere along the line it is bound to dawn on you. You know it is not taking you anywhere.

But the hope keeps you going—the hope that one day through the same thing you will probably reach your goal—because that instrument (i.e. thought) is born out of time, is born out of cause and effect, and it cannot conceive of anything except in terms of time. So if time is not there, there is nothing to happen—let alone in the future—because it is time that has created the need for the timeless. *Time* means the future. If this time is cut off, it is not as if what you expect to happen will happen now. There is nothing to happen here. Time burns itself out when the timeless is knocked off.

Whatever you want to happen is in terms of time. Assuming for a moment that you are already in the blissful state, you don't want to be in that state tomorrow. Whatever the state you want to be in, you are not in that state, because the goal is there, which is tomorrow, not today. So if this (goal) is not there, the thought that is thinking in terms of something happening in time is not there. Unfortunately, there is nothing to happen. Happening is in time. When time is not there, there is no happening, nothing to happen there. Atman is Brahman—that is exactly what it means. The Brahman you want in the future is already here; there is nothing to happen here. Achieving (it doesn't matter what you call it) is in time, so it is bound to be caught up in cause and effect. You want to produce a result, but this is not a result, not a happening, not an achievement.

Anything you do with this will cause you pain. That is why I say the search for moksha [liberation] is the dukkha [suffering] of all dukkhas. [laughter] There's no end to that. You will keep searching for this eternally; you are not going to get it. Even if you get what you want, and experience bliss, beatitude, God knows what, there is always more and more of it. Silence you experience, but you want permanent silence, you want always to be in silence. But in the very nature of things, there is no permanence at all. You have never lived with these liberated people. (I do not know if there are any.)

It's a very simple thing. It's so simple that the complex structure does not want to leave it alone. There's nothing that you can do, of course; you are condemned. [laughs] You are condemned.

So leave it alone.

Leave it alone.

We can't do that either.

You don't seem to be able to do that either.

If we can leave it alone, then we have done everything.

Then there's nothing to happen.

We wouldn't be here if we had left it alone. But he said, "You don't get any-thing by coming here."

You can stay with that man all your life. Nothing is going to happen.

We haven't realized that nothing we can do...

You cannot say, "There isn't anything that I can do." You see, the moment you come to that point—"There isn't anything that I can do about it!"—then you don't have to do anything. No outside agency can be of any help.

Nor the inside agency?

Then there is no inside there, no outside. The inside is always related to the outside, you understand?
  So you don't even complete the sentence, "There isn't anything that I can do about it." Even before the completion of that sentence, "There isn't anything I can do about it," [snaps his fingers] it has done the trick. The triggering apparatus is part of you; it's there.

I have what may seem like a silly question. Do you practice meditation?

Nothing—no meditations—nothing. What is there to meditate upon? I discovered all those things before—the mantras, the meditations, what meditation does. I didn't practice, of course, Transcendental

Meditation or any such thing, but some meditations. So, this I discovered for myself: Meditation is a self-centered activity. It is strengthening the very self you want to be free from. What are you meditating for? You want to be free from something. What are you to meditate on? All right, thought is a noise, sound. What is sound? You look at this and you say, "This is a tape-recorder," so thought is sound. There is a continuous flow of thoughts, and you are linking up all these thoughts all the time, and this is the noise you can't stand. Why can't you stand that noise? So, by repeating mantras, you create a louder noise, and you submerge the noise of thought, and then you are at peace with yourself. You think that something marvelous is happening to you. But all meditation is a self-centered activity.

I don't talk of a meditative state. That is Krishnamurti's business. He talks about a meditative state: "It is not this; it is not that." All right, if this is a meditative state, what am I meditating upon? I am meditating upon that [indicates some object] at this moment, looking at that. The reflecting of that is here. Something is moving; life is movement. All the time something or other is happening there—all the time—and the movement there is the movement here. There is no moment when something or other is not happening. In the night everything is silent for a moment, or you hear the lizards making noises. You have to listen to them. If there is no noise of any kind around you, you have to listen to the "lub-dub" of your heart, or to the flow of your blood through your veins like a river. That is noise. You can delude yourself and imagine that it is omkara [the mystical sound *om*]. It is not omkara. This body is a machine. The human machine produces noise just as a running car engine does. Why do you have to say it is omkara, brahmanadam, and all that? It is the noise of the human machine. You will go crazy if you listen to the "lub-dub-lub-dub" of your own heart. But that is all there is to listen to here unless some other thing is happening—somebody coughing, somebody snoring, or somebody having nightmares.

There is not one moment of boredom for this man. For hours and hours I can sit here and watch the clock pendulum moving there. I can't be bored. I really don't know what it is. The pendulum is moving there. The whole of my being is that movement. For hours and hours I can sit here and look at it. You are not interested in that thing. You are interested in something else, some meditation. This individual is always in a state of meditation. "Where is that movement?" I am wondering. That is the meditation that is going on. Not that I am wondering in the usual sense of the word—this individual remains in a state of wonder for the rest of his life. *Outside* and *inside* are created by thought. When there is no movement of thought, you don't know whether it is inside or outside. This is just like a mirror. This is a live mirror reflecting things exactly as they are. There is nobody here. I don't see anything; the whole of my body is reflecting things exactly the way they are out there.

The recognizing and naming mechanism is in the background except when there is a need for it. This absence of the movement of thought, which recognizes and names things, is the state of samadhi, sahaja [natural] samadhi. You imagine that samadhi is something he goes into and comes out of. Not at all; he's always there. Whether the eyes of such a man are open or closed, he does not know what he is looking at.

A person who has come into such a state of samadhi is like a madman and a child rolled into one. Madcaps function in exactly the same way. The thoughts are disconnected, disjointed things, and so the actions are also disconnected, the feelings are also disconnected. But their thoughts are accompanied by hallucinations, mental images, seeing something that isn't there. That's the only difference. This state is always a state of wonder. He doesn't know what he is looking at, he doesn't know what he is smelling, and yet his senses are working at their peak capacities, extraordinarily sensitive, taking in everything.

Why am I not in the state you are describing?

Because there is a constant demand on your part to experience everything that you look at, everything that you are feeling inside. Constantly, because if you don't do that, you are coming to an end. "You" as you know yourself, you as you experience yourself, are coming to an end, and you do not want that to come to an end. You want the continuity. So all spiritual pursuits are in the direction of strengthening that continuity. It's a self-centered activity. Through self-centered activity, how can you be free from the activities of the "self"? So all your experiences, all your meditations, all your sadhana, all that you do is a self-centered activity. It is strengthening the self, it is adding momentum, gathering momentum, so it is taking you in the opposite direction. Whatever you do to be free from the self also is a self-centered activity. You can't divide these things into two. The process you adopt to reach what you call *being* is also a becoming process. I don't know if I make myself clear. So there is no such thing as being and becoming. You are always in the becoming process, no matter what you call it. If you want to be yourself and not somebody else, that also is a becoming process. There is nothing to do about this. Anything you do to put yourself in that state of being is a becoming process. That is all that I am pointing out.

It can never lead to the being process?

No, anything you do, any movement in any direction on any level is a self-centered activity. That is a very clever thing. It has survived for centuries. It knows all the tricks in the world.

How could this illusion of an entity called the self have remained with us all these millennia, in spite of all these people who have gotten whatever it is, realization and all that?

How? [laughs] It is there. It is there. Every time you do something, whether it is a good deed or a bad deed, you are strengthening that. You see, we are all functioning in this "thought sphere," if I may use those words. What you pick out of that thought sphere is your particular background, your culture, so it's like an antenna. The antenna is the product of the culture. You pick up thoughts that are beneficial to you to protect thought. Thought is a protective mechanism. What is it that it is protecting? It is protecting itself. It will do everything possible to prevent itself from breaking up. So even if you introduce the so-called spiritual pursuits, it is only the strengthening of that. It is not in the opposite direction, so you are on the wrong track. There is neither a positive nor a negative approach. The so-called negative approach also is a positive approach. Any approach, all approaches, whether you call them negative or positive or whatever—they are approaches. So there is no approach; there is nothing that you can do.

You have adopted the negative approach because your positive approaches have proved to be very frustrating. You feel there is a distinction between the two. But even what you call the negative approach is a positive approach. You turn it into a positive approach because the goal you want to reach is a positive goal. You want to achieve something, you want to accomplish something, to attain God knows what—the state of not knowing—through a negative approach.

The negative approach has to negate itself by itself. This is not a negative approach with a positive goal, with the idea of arriving at some conclusion. I am always negating what I am saying. I make a statement, but that statement is not expressing all that is being said, so I negate it. You say I am contradicting myself. I am not contradictory at all. I negate the first statement, the second statement, and all the other statements. That is why sometimes it sounds very contradictory. I am negating it all the time, not with the idea of arriving at any point, just negating. There is no purpose in my talking. I am only pointing out the basic situation that you cannot understand what I am talking about. It is not possible for you to listen to me without interpreting. I am all the time trying to knock off the reference point. When the reference point is absent, there is no need to understand me, you understand? I am all the time saying that. The old chappie talks of the "art of listening," the "real listening," and you think there is a way to listen, an art of listening. There's nothing like that at all. You won't even know what I am talking about.

You are not in a position to accept or reject what I am saying. You accept a statement because it fits your reference point, your assumptions like self-realization, God-realization, etc. The reference point is you. There is nothing other than the reference point there. That is you. If the reference point goes, you go with it. That is the end of you.

Your very listening is interpretation. You never listen to anybody. It is not possible for you to listen to anybody without interpreting. The interpretation is a part of your background, you see, so it is not possible for you to listen to anything without interpreting what you are listening to.

So, is there any other listening? There is a listening quite independent of words, but that is not on the conscious level. (It does not mean that you are unconscious. I must make it very clear.) That is a pure and simple physical response to the sound. The sound sets in motion the tympanum, so it is just a vibration. You really don't know what he is talking about. This is a physiological phenomenon, so I express this only in physiological terms. Not in psychological, not in religious, not in spiritual terms, because it's very important for me to express this state in pure and simple physical and physiological terms.

If you play back a tape of this conversation, it will make no sense to me. Yesterday I was listening to a tape of me talking in Bangalore. "What is this fellow saying? All this is meaningless twaddle. I wouldn't listen to that chap." That tape is a dead thing. It may be my words, but it has no meaning to me. Forget it! Burn it! Throw it away! This is just a machine responding to the stimuli of your questions. You have created the problem of their "answers"; I am not involved. I have no commitment to consistency. I have no viewpoint to put forward, no thesis to expound. I only respond to your stimulus.

When you ask a question, it is picked up immediately. I don't even decode it. Before you have even asked the question, the answer is there. You can do it; it is nothing unusual. If you are not preoccupied with anything of your own, it is an easy thing. It is not thought reading. It is just an echo chamber. What is going on there is going on here. You can't do that. You want to decode every thought, to translate everything.

What I'm saying can't be experienced by you except through the help of thought. In other words, as long as movement of thought is there, it is not possible for you to understand what I'm talking about. When it is not there, there is no need for you to understand. In that sense, there is nothing to understand.

Life is one unitary movement, not two different movements. It's moving, it's a continuous flux, but you cannot look at that flux and say, "That is a flux." Then why do I say this is a flux? It is only to give you a feel about it that I use those words. But if you translate these words in terms of your concepts and abstractions, you are lost. Really, you do not know a thing about what is being said. You don't understand at all. So, if you realize that, what happens? Then there is no movement of thought there. (Wanting to understand means there is a movement of thought.) You really don't know a thing about what this chap is saying. Then, what happens inside of you is only that you repeat these phrases, phrase by phrase, word by word, without translating them, without interpreting them in terms of your concepts. His talking is just a noise. You are an echo chamber there; that's all that happens. You are not there. (When the "you" is there, you are translating.) This is just a pure and simple physiological functioning of the organism. Because there is life, there is a response. The response and the stimulus are not two different movements. You cannot separate the response from the stimulus. (The moment you separate the response from the stimulus, there is a division. It is a divisive consciousness that is in operation.) So, it is one movement.

Thought and life are one interfluent movement. But there seems to be a movement of thought, parallel to the movement of life, going on in you all the time. There seems to be; otherwise there would be no need for us to sit and talk about this. Listening to me, or trying to understand me, would not be there. If there were no continuity of thought in you, this situation that we have created for ourselves in this room wouldn't exist any more. You wouldn't want to listen to any chap describing how he is functioning. Why should you? If he is functioning that way, all right, jolly good. Why are you interested in that? Why do you establish any relationship?

As long as you listen to me, you are lost. You listen to me because you want to understand what I am talking about. Not that it is something abstract or difficult, but your understanding is through the thinking instrument, and that is not the instrument to understand this. The refined, sensitized instrument, you call *intuition,* but there is no other instrument. If that is not the instrument and there is no other instrument, the logical conclusion from that statement is: Is there anything to understand? There is nothing to understand.

That understanding is here somehow. I don't know how it came. That is why I cannot take you there. It has no cause. You are interested in finding out the cause because you want it to happen in you. Otherwise you would not be interested in the cause.

So it is not a question of understanding me. It is not possible to understand me. It is just not possible to understand. The only thing you can understand is within that framework and in relation to that reference point. You think that the more you listen, the more these things become clear to you, but the clarity of thought is making it more difficult for you to understand what I am talking about. So you come back year after year, and you think things are becoming clearer and clearer for you, but actually it is destroying the possibility of understanding anything.

There is nothing to understand. That understanding somehow is there, and how it came about nobody knows, and there is no way at all of making you see this. You ask, "Why do you talk?" You come here. As long as you think that you can see more and more clearly, I say you have seen nothing. J. Krishnamurti says, "Seeing is the end." If you say you have seen, you have not seen, because seeing is the end of the structure that says that. There is no seeing you can know. In other words, there is no seeing. As long as you think you can understand this more, see the world around you more clearly, I say you will see nothing and understand nothing. This conversation is not going to get you anywhere. My only interest is to end all this.

The difference between you and me is that you are trying to understand. The absence of what is going on there is what is here. Discussion only adds to the confusion; it is completely useless. I can only point out the obstacle, that's all.

Is this some kind of preparation?

It is not. I repeat endlessly, "Inquiry is useless," but you want to apply the techniques you have learned in life to this. You say, "Buddha sat under a tree and said he would not move." He had done everything and realized that nothing could help him. He knew that nothing could help him, and probably something happened then. You argue, "He did this, so why can't I follow the same path?" But it is totally different for you. You are not in that position; you still hope something will happen. The point is that there is nothing to understand.

When you say, "I don't know a thing," does it not imply that you know?

You see, it is not that I know I am in a state of not knowing. The statement, "I don't know a thing," is an expression of that state. Be very clear about it. It is not that I say to myself that I don't know what I am looking at. That state is throwing out the expression "I don't know." That is the expression, the description of the state by itself. Not that there is somebody who is saying "I don't know"—the state itself says, by itself, "I really don't know a thing about it." It is so!

"It is so" sounds like a dogmatic statement.

When all attempts and efforts on your part fail to fit what is being said into the logical framework, the rational framework, I have to say that you cannot in any way understand what it is all about. It is beyond logic, it is beyond rationality, it is so. You have to accept or reject the statement that I don't know a thing about it. It is not a positive statement. You can never experience it. Don't try! That is not going to help you at all. It is so. There are no two ways about it. Not that I am being dogmatic. It is not a dogmatic statement. I really don't know a thing. It is so, because you, the structure trying to understand, are not going to understand. In that sense, it is so. It is so here. I can't understand a thing about it. It is so here; it must be so there also. It is not so there, because you are still trying to understand, experience, something that you can never understand.

There is a difficulty of understanding here. (We are using such simple English. The sages talked at a time when words had completely different meanings. There were no tape-recorders, no stenographers. Their students listened and passed it on.) That is why I often ask, "What is my teaching? Please tell me." I don't know a thing about my teaching. I don't know a thing about my state—not that I can. I know I cannot. The limitation is there. It has its own limitation, and it has understood its limitation. It cannot experience that at all; that's all I am saying. Since I don't know a thing about my state, I can't make any statement, either positive or negative, because both positive and negative statements are within the field of thought. But you are saying a lot about my state. You seem to know a lot more about my state than I do. How can you say anything about my state? You are not saying anything about my state. All this is an interpretation of what I am saying. You see, your very listening is an interpretation. You cannot listen to what I am saying. If you are in that state where there is just an echo of what I am saying, repeating the words without understanding them, you really don't know what this chap is talking about, and you don't even try to understand. If there were any listening, all that you are saying would be absent. That is why I say you are not listening.

I am telling you the simple fact that you cannot listen to me at all. Your listening to me or not is not the point. You cannot listen to what I am saying at all. Whatever you make out of your listening is your own listening, not what I am saying. What I am saying, you don't know, I don't know. [laughter] I am not saying anything about that at all. The only thing I am saying is that you are not listening, because you can't listen. You can't listen, so don't try! That's all I am saying.

What I am saying has no logic. If it has a logic, it has a logic of its own. I don't know anything about it. But you have necessarily to fit me into the logical structure of your thought. Otherwise the logical structure there, the rational thing, comes to an end. You see, you have to rationalize; that is what you are. But this has nothing to do with rationality. It has nothing to do with your logic. That doesn't mean that it is illogical or irrational.

What do you want to understand? There is nothing to understand; that is the understanding I am talking about. If you understand what it is all about, what I am talking about, you are already there. It will be something new, something totally new. You will give expression to it in a completely different way. You will not repeat what Buddha said, what Jesus said, what JK said, or what some other Krishnamurti is saying. It will be new, and it will express itself in a totally different way. How will it express itself? I don't know, you don't know, nobody knows. If others fit me into their frameworks, it is their business. We do not have any vested interest in that.

You will probably fit me into some framework and that so-and-so said this before. That is my misfortune wherever I go. Krishnamurti people come, Ramana Maharshi people come, others come, and they say, "You are saying the same thing!" How the hell do you know I am saying the same thing? Do you know anything of what he is talking about? First of all you must know what he is talking about and what is there behind it, and then you can compare what I am saying with what he is saying. I am not saying any of those things.

I don't compare myself with anybody. Why compare myself with sages, saints, and saviors? It would be the biggest tragedy of my life, wouldn't it? I don't compare myself at all. What I am saying is not the same thing that has been said before. No. How do I know? You see, you are trying to fit me into that framework. You have necessarily to do that. If you don't do that, you come to an end. That is a dangerous point. So you have to reject me totally, saying, "He is talking some nonsense, rubbish, bosh!" Or you have to fit me into whatever particular background you have, or into somebody else's framework, and say, "He is saying the same thing." Otherwise the tin gods you have created out of somebody's teaching will collapse. You have necessarily to do that—either one or the other.

Sir, what is your message?

It is quite simple. You are not going to get anything here. You are wasting your time. Pack up and go! That is my message. I have nothing to give. You have nothing to take. If you continue to sit there, you are wasting your time. The one thing you have to do is get up and go. If you still think I can give you something, you'll have to sit there until kingdom come. I have nothing to give. There's nothing to be given.

The holy business—I am not in it. I don't want a thing. I have nothing to give, so there's no breach of contract here. Nothing. I don't want anything. You may think that I am talking for self-fulfillment. If I do, that will be my tragedy, my misery. So you are out. You are not interested in involving yourself in my tragedy.

Are you here for lokasangraha [uplifting the world?]

I am not here for lokasangraha. I do not give a damn for you. I know you are doomed. If you think something is going to happen, and sit here day after day, week after week, year after year, waiting till kingdom come, even then no kingdom will come. Go where you will, and do what you want! I tell you very clearly, loud and clear, in clear, unmistakable language, that there is nothing to be communicated now or at any time. I am really surprised. In spite of that assertive statement, you hang on here. It is your funeral. You are chasing something that does not exist. There is nothing to be transformed, nothing to be changed, nothing to be understood. So long as you want to be like me, you will remain what you are, asking the same questions. You will get the same answer. The one answer for all questions is, "Stop asking questions!"
How do you think people should be?

They can't be any different than what they are. A murderer will remain a murderer. Of course, he has to pay the price. You have outlawed murder, and still it is on the increase. I see a murderer lurking in you. If you can't get what you want, and someone stands in the way of what you want, and you want it that badly, then you will not hesitate to remove that person by any means. That is all. All your talk of culture does not mean a thing to me. The whole culture is built on the foundation of kill and get killed. They are even teaching that in the universities. I am not afraid of you. You can murder me; it is your privilege.

You can't be other than what you are. Whatever you are trying to do to change, you will not succeed. Stop running away from yourself! What is the good of my saying so? There is no use my telling you that, because you are not going to stop it. I am telling you to stop it. You are not certain of it: "Maybe there is something that can be done." I am certain that you have no freedom of action. In that sense I go a step further and say that you are genetically controlled. Naturally you will say that that statement is a theory. You have a hope that you can do something. There are many people in the holy business who assure you that you can do something, so you will go there—as simple as that. My certainty remains. You call it a theory. All right, you can go and try your luck. In the end you will find out for yourself and by yourself, "That chappie is right!" I'll sing my song and go.

On my side it is very clear. There are so many people who have said they can help you. You would do well to go there and try your luck. But I want to add this statutory warning (like the one you have on the cigarette packs): You are not going to get anything from anybody, because there is nothing to get. That is why I say that since there is no such thing as enlightenment, the question whether X or Y is enlightened or not does not at all arise. You are all like-minded people who are after such things, that is all. That is your projection, your ideation about those people, that is all that I am saying. There may not be anything there other than what you have projected on them.

Is a person in the natural state compassionate?

That is your projection. They are callous, indifferent, unconcerned. Compassion is one of the gimmicks of the holy business, sales talk. Do you think this individual is conscious that he is full of compassion? If he is, it is not compassion. You are giving the names. How does it operate? You tell me. What kind of compassion do you see in him? It is your assumption that I am compassionate.

This is not a thing to be talked about and praised. If you start an organization, ninety per cent of what they collect will be used up by the administration. So many organizations are there in America. All the rich, social women go and collect funds, and ninety per cent of the funds are used up in administration. That is all you can do. You are not going to change the world. You are not called upon to change this world.

I am not interested in changing the society. What I am saying has absolutely no social content at all. What is wrong with this world? Why do you want to change the world? This is an extraordinarily beautiful world! You want to change this world so that you can live in a world of your own ideas. The real problem is that you want to change yourself, and you find it's impossible, and so you want to change the world so that you can fit the world into your own pattern.

Is there no social content there? They talk of lokasangraha. They mean that the presence of a realized man purifies. He gives out pure vibrations, and the atmosphere is cleansed.

Has it? Has it really? More blood has been shed in the name of the man who talked about loving thy neighbor as thyself, than in all the recent wars put together. Do you call that social content? They are all fighting, quarrelling. How can there be any social content? You want to be a good man, a nice man, an innocent man, and all that stuff. You want to be something different, always tomorrow or the day after. But even then you will say exactly the same thing—the next life. That is what all the teachers promise you (and they just promise you)—next life. Till then he is in business, he is assured. If he says there is nothing, you leave him. That is why I do not have to bother. You are going to leave in any case, because what brings you here will certainly take you somewhere else. You are interested in getting something. You are not going to get it. There is some kind of a false hope or promise. I don't give false hopes or promises. But they have created some hope, so you go on and on and on. Like riding a tiger, you can't get off.

There's no journey. Both are kidding themselves—those who take or pretend to take you on the journey, and those who are trying. You can't walk with me. How can you walk with me? You are so frightened of the thorns there, the stones. You want a trained guide. I myself don't know the terrain. Have you never heard of the proverb that warns you never to walk with a man who has sandals, because he always walks on thorns? You will get into trouble. I myself do not know the terrain; I am just going.

You can talk of so many things—home truths. "Be good. Be wise." But this has no social content at all. This cannot be used to change the world, reform the world, create a new man, a new world. All that is balderdash. Maybe some people do it just to help some people. That's all right. Do something. If it works, it works. But to suggest something like that, knowing very well that it is not going to work, is not right. "Let's give them some new toys to play with. All the traditional things have failed, so here are some new toys, specially imported from Japan." What are you doing? You are not doing anything. You are repeating new phrases, new words, new idioms. That is all you are doing.

You don't accept the fact that all that is a contamination there in that consciousness. Whatever you consider sacred, whatever you consider extraordinary—Buddha Consciousness, Christ Consciousness, Krishna Consciousness—is a contamination in that consciousness. It has to purify itself. All that dross—all that is holy, all that is sacred—must go. When that has gone, you are yourself. Otherwise there is dependence. You experience something extraordinary there and start an organization, Krishna Consciousness or some other. These organizations collect twenty million dollars and publish books so that they can transmit, make others experience, those silly things.

Is there any difference between going to a church and coming here?

Basically the motivation is the same. You are looking for a new teacher, a new Bible, a new order, a new Church. That is all you can do. Basically it's still the same thing. You have not moved one step from the Catholic Church. If religiousness is all you are interested in, there is no need to look anywhere other than in Christianity. The profound statements of the great teachers are not any different in the different religions. All I am saying is that looking to alien lands and religions does not mean anything. You learn new techniques, new systems, new phrases, and then you begin to think and speak in terms of this new language, and probably you feel just great, but basically it does not mean anything at all.

You have shattered all my young dreams.

No, no, you cannot be so sure; they are still there. There is a very powerful plaster. If there is a little crack in your structure, you will plaster it over. It is very powerful. It has millions and millions of years of momentum. It knows all the tricks. It can invent any trick to gain momentum. That is its nature. There isn't anything you can do about it. You can discuss it for forty years, but I promise you, you will not get anywhere. If anyone makes you believe you can get somewhere, he's taking you for a ride. He may be honest. Distrust all honest fellows! Throw them out! There is no one who is honest in this field. No outside agency can help you.

You totally discard the teachings of the swamis [holy men]?

I am not discarding. I am telling you, "Go to a swami and he will give you something. What you want, he will give you. Good luck!" That is all. I can tell you that you are not going to get this at all. It is not something that you can get. I wish you the best of luck. I know very well that it is not something that you or anybody else can get or that anybody can give. I can't give it. If there is somebody who promises, he is just promising, and he is going to take you for a long ride. He is just kidding you. He cannot deliver the goods, so he says, "Next life" or "Ten years hence." He is safe.

What do you ask us to do? What should we do?

I am not asking you to do anything. My problem is that I really don't know where you are. I can't help you in that matter; you have to tell me. Where are you? What makes you think that you are different from me? I am not different from you; I can't be.

You can't be interested in this. How can you be interested in this? That is my question. How can you be interested in this kind of a thing? What you are interested in is a totally different thing, fancy stuff, fantasy. You may indulge in all kinds of fantasy; that's your affair. If this is not fantasy, you will be interested in some other kind of fantasy. How can you be interested in liquidating yourself? That is my question. All that you know—"you" as you know yourself, you as you experience yourself—is interested in continuity. It knows all the tricks. You cannot beat that.

People ask the question. All questions reduce themselves to the one question—"How? How am I going to get what you have? How?" And through "How?" that structure is permanently establishing itself there and getting its continuity. "How?" There is no how. If you are interested in how, those swamis will help you.

The people who remain with you for some time are not, by and large, the kind of people I enjoy being with. Association with you seems to encourage lack of generosity, coldness, smugness. I like people who are warm, outgoing, affectionate.

I am not interested in the whole field of self-expression, getting in touch with one's feelings, overcoming inhibitions and so on. I respond to what people come to see me about, the natural state. If people are interested in psychological change, so-called consciousness expansion and all that, let them go to encounter groups, or see psychiatrists and engage in what I call the Freudian fraud. In the end their so-called growth will not bring them happiness and neither will their improved sex lives (if their sex lives improve). At best they will simply have learned to be unhappy in a new and richer way. I am not concerned with that. My interest is in the subject they come to see me about in the first place. My interest is in pointing out the utter impossibility of doing anything whatsoever to attain the natural state.

Anyhow, the people who come to see me do not stay very long. They come a few times or hang around for a few months, then they either go back to their ordinary lives or go on to some fellow who promises them what they seek. Some of them become devotees of Bubba Free John, the latest American avatar. Either way, that's fine with me.

But one thing I will never do is deceive them. I will never suggest in any way that I can give them anything. I will never hook them into some phony baloney idea about practicing undifferentiated awareness and the observer being the same as the observed, and all that.

So it's okay with you if your followers are dreary and uptight?

Everything is okay with me. If you have a million dollars and eight girl friends, that's okay with me. If you are lonely and disagreeable and penniless and dying of cancer, that also is okay with me. I am perfectly happy with everything as it is. I am happy with misery, poverty, and death. I am also happy with wealth and psychological fulfillment. I think the solution to your real problems is, in any case, not possible for you unless you undergo the sort of biological transformation that has happened to me. Which is not to say that I ever consider myself superior to you or to anyone else because of this. Quite the contrary, the idea of superiority or inferiority never even enters my head for one moment. The total absence of this idea is one of the characteristics of this whole transformation business.

If you were to sum up your teaching in one phrase, what would it be?

The phrase would be, "I cannot help you."

Still, people do come to see you, both here in Switzerland and in India. You must help them in some way, or they must think you help them in some way, otherwise they wouldn't come.

Some come out of curiosity. But to those who come because they seriously wish to understand me, all I can say is, I have nothing to say. I cannot help anyone at all, and neither can anyone else. You do not need help. On the contrary, you need to be totally helpless. And if you seek to achieve this helplessness through my help, you are lost.

Can you speak of the difference between your state and the state of being of most people?

I think it is very slight; there is only a hair's breadth difference.
But your body has undergone biological changes.

Yes, but I have no secret hidden in a secret place. I have nothing to offer. All I can offer is the assurance that all inquiry, like all philosophical discussion, is useless, that no dialogue is possible, and that your questions, like everyone else's, serve no purpose whatsoever.

Understanding, in the sense in which I mean it, is that state of being where the questions aren't there any more.

You mean it is a state of not thinking?

It is a state where thinking and life are not two things, but one thing. It is not an intellectual state; it is more like a state of feeling (although I use the word *feeling* in a different sense than that in which you use the word). It is a state of not seeking. Man is always seeking something— money, power, sex, love, mystical experience, truth, enlightenment— and it is this seeking which keeps him out of his natural state. And although I am in a natural state, I cannot help someone else, because it is my natural state, not his.

Do you mean to say that if I stop seeking, a change will take place in me?

Yes, it will. And when I've said, "Yes, it will," then what? What good is my assurance to you? It is not good at all. It is utterly worthless, so you don't listen to me or anybody. Listening to other people is what you've been doing all your life. It's the cause of your unhappiness. You are unique. There is no reason for your wanting to be like another chap. You can't be like him, anyway. This wanting—wanting to listen, wanting to understand, wanting to be like such-and-such an individual— has come about because society is interested in creating a perfect man. But there is no such thing as a perfect man; this is our problem. All we can do is be ourselves, and no one can help you be that. He can teach you how to ski or fix a motorcar, but he cannot teach you anything important.

Not even Buddha or Christ?

Why do you bother about those fellows? They are dead. You should pitch them in the river. And yet you don't. You keep listening to someone (it makes no difference whom), and you keep hoping that somehow, tomorrow or the next day, by listening more and more, you will get off the merry-go-round. You listen to your parents and to your teachers at school, and they tell you to be good and dutiful and not be angry and so on, and that doesn't do any good, and so you go and learn how to do Yoga, and then presently some old chap comes along and tells you to be choicelessly aware. Or maybe you find someone in the holy business and he does miracles. He produces some trinkets out of the air, and you fall for it. Or perhaps he touches you, and you see some blue light or green light or yellow light or God knows what, and you hope he will help you experience enlightenment. But he cannot help you. It is not something that can be captured, contained, or given expression to. I do not know if you see the utter helplessness of the situation, and how, if anyone thinks he can help you, he will inevitably mislead you. And the less phony he is, the more powerful he is, the more enlightened he is, the more misery and mischief he will create for you.

Have you any interest in the question of reincarnation?

I am more interested in the question, "Are you born?" Can you tell me? You yourself—can you be sure that you are born? Can you experience your own birth? You cannot. You can experience the births of others and the deaths of others, and you think that some day you will experience your own death. But there is no guarantee you will experience your own death. Your structure that is interested in understanding your own death and your own birth won't be there. So life as such has no beginning and no end. It is a beginningless and endless movement, and you are only an expression of it. You are only an expression of life, like a bird or a worm or a cloud.

But with the singular difference that I am conscious of myself, and the worm is not.

You are conscious of yourself through thought, by which I mean not just conscious thought, but that conditioning that transforms the life that passes through you into feelings, into pleasure and pain. And this thought is not yours. It is what you have learned from others, it is second-hand, it belongs to everybody. You belong to everybody. So why don't you accept the natural thing? If you accept the natural thing, all falls into its own rhythm. There is nothing to do, there is nothing to control, there is nothing to ask. You don't have to do a thing. You are finished.

Well, one can't just sit on a hill and rot.

Still rotting, no matter where you are. Not necessarily on a hill—right in the midst of all your activities the rotting is going on. And the burden is that you can one day, somehow, through some miracle or through the help of somebody, do something about it. You can't do a thing about it, let's face it. No miracles! Nobody can help you!

So, if nobody can help...

And you do not know how to help yourself. That's the point. You know, these two are not different things. If you really come to the point that no outside agency can be of any help, automatically your total helplessness also goes. These are the obverse and reverse of the same coin. You still have some hope. The fact that you are here means you have not given up hope. Or, if you don't come here, you will go to see somebody else in India—the avatar himself, the god himself walking on the Earth. Probably he will produce some trinkets out of thin air, but what good is that? No matter who he is, if you had no hope, you wouldn't listen to him, you wouldn't touch a book, you wouldn't listen to anybody in this world. Not that you would be proud or anything, but all outside agency in any form, on any level, would be finished once and for all.

"I don't know what to do. I am helpless, totally helpless." As long as you think you are totally helpless, you will depend on some outside agency. That can be finished in one stroke. In one blow your dependence on outside agencies is finished, and, along with it, the idea that you are helpless, that you don't know what to do about it, is also gone. But you are waiting for something to happen or for some grace to descend upon you. You are still depending upon some outside agency. I can tell you that there is no power outside of you—no power. This does not mean that you have all the attributes that you read about of the super-duper gods, but there is no power outside of you. If there is any power in this universe, it is in you.

I'm convinced of what you say.

It's not a question of conviction. It's a fact, and that fact cannot be experienced by you. As long as you say to yourself that you are convinced, you are not so sure.

There's no power outside of me, here and now?

You don't let that power express itself, because that's a thing that you cannot experience. You want to experience it. How is that possible? That power is something living, vital. It's the throb, the pulse, the beat of life. You are one expression of that life, that's all. How can you experience that? This structure of thought, through which you experience, is dead. It cannot experience that life at all, because the one is something living and the other is dead, and there can't be any relationship between the two. You can only experience dead things, not a living thing. Life has to express itself. This is a thing that nobody can teach you. You don't have to get it from somebody. What you have is there.

Yes. But if...

There is no "Yes. But..." You can't say *yes* and begin the next sentence with *but*. There is no *but* there. If the *yes* is a real *yes*, that releases the thing there. The *yes* fades into nothingness and then what is there begins to express itself. If you say *but*, you are giving continuity to that dead structure of thought, experience and hope. *Yes!* is the thing that blows the whole structure apart.

No outside agency can help you—nobody—not even this chap who is talking so much about all this. He cannot help you. (At least he is honest: "All right, I cannot help.") So all outside agencies are finished. That is a very difficult point to arrive at. "All outside agencies are finished for me!" You don't go and listen to anybody, no matter however holy he may be. He may be the God of Gods. He may say, "I have come to liberate the whole of mankind!" But you don't go there, you understand? (If you go there just to satisfy your curiosity, that's a different matter.) You don't seek anything from any source outside. So you fall back on yourself, and you really don't know. You want to find out. You ask the question again and again. You are stuck with it. "How can I understand this thing?" When you are finished with all answers from outside and no answer is forthcoming from inside, what happens to that question? That question cannot remain there. It dissolves itself. Ionization of thought takes place because it cannot escape, and that is energy, that is life.

We hear you spent seven years with J. Krishnamurti. Do you mean to say his influence has no bearing on your present state? It is a big zero for you?

Absolutely. Some people come and ask me, "You hung around Krishnamurti for seven years. Do you mean to say that it had no impact?" I say, "In spite of Krishnamurti, this thing happened." If it has to happen, it has to happen in spite of me and in spite of my teachers. No impact, nothing. On the contrary, it made it very difficult for me. I can say that it prevents and destroys the possibility of being yourself, of unburdening yourself of your past.

How can you unburden yourself of the past? The word *unburden* implies there is something that you can do to unburden yourself. There is nothing you can do to free yourself from the past. This is only a description of the state where the past does not operate anymore. It cannot influence your actions. Those actions are not your actions anymore. You don't know anything about that action. It is a thing that cannot be manipulated by you at all, the action of life itself. At the same time I want to point out that it is not a mystical or religious thing or a pure, spontaneous action. It has nothing to do with that. Life is acting all the time, in the sense that as long as sensory activity is in operation, something is happening. Not one, but millions and millions of sensations are hitting the human organism. This human organism is not separate from that. It is one electromagnetic field. It is one field, and what isolates and separates you and creates a tiny electromagnetic field is thought.

Can one uncondition one's thought through being aware of it?
How do you see the thought? Have you really tried this, or have you just accepted the idea? The one who is looking at conditioned thought is also conditioned, so do you see the absurdity of doing this? I don't think so. You can't do a thing. Don't get on this journey of freeing yourself from the conditioning of your own thought.

But you are still trying. You accept these ideas. You never question the validity of those statements. It doesn't matter who says it, it is false for you. Not only that, it is falsifying you because you do not test the validity of those statements for yourself.

The conditioning, you see—you will never be free from that. Don't believe anybody. There is no such thing as an unconditioned mind. The mind is conditioned. If there is a mind, it is bound to be conditioned. There is no such thing as an open mind. In the Theosophical Society we used to repeat, "an open mind." How absurd that statement is! Mind can never be open; it is a closed thing. I don't accept that there is such a thing as the mind, let alone the open mind or the unconditioned mind. There is no totality of these thoughts and experiences. They are all disconnected, disjointed things.

The thoughtless state, silence—how can you experience silence? That's my question. How can you experience the thoughtless state? You'll never be free from thought. If there is any such thing as a thoughtless state, it can never be experienced by you or by anybody. Whatever you experience there is created by this thought.

We used to write essays, "Time and the Timeless," ridiculous stuff. It is time that creates the timeless and then pursues the timeless. And through this pursuit, time is continuing. Continuity is all that it is interested in.

Abstractions are very misleading. If you start talking in terms of "innocence," in terms of this, that, and the other, you are lost. Abstractions are very misleading, very misleading. You talk of innocence. What do you know about that innocence? In that state you really don't know what you are looking at. You don't know that you are looking at your wife. Can there be any relationship? Can there be a wife? Can there be children? You see, you can talk of innocence, but when there is no mind, why talk of the innocent mind? Where is the mind, or the unconditioned mind? These phrases are very misleading. They are not going to help in any way.

To me there is no such thing as mind; mind is a myth. Since there is no such thing as mind, the "mutation of mind" that J. Krishnamurti is talking about has no meaning. There is nothing there to be transformed, radically or otherwise. There is no self to be realized. The whole religious structure that has been built on this foundation collapses because there is nothing there to realize. To me, Krishnamurti is playing exactly the same game as all those ugly saints in the market whom we have in the world today. Krishnamurti's teaching is phony baloney. There is nothing to his teaching at all, and he cannot produce anything at all. A person may listen to him for sixty, seventy, or a hundred years, but nothing will ever happen to that man, because the whole thing is phony. If the number of followers is the criterion of a successful spiritual teacher, JK is a pygmy. He's a mere wordsmith. He has created a new trap.

You want to smoke cigarettes, and there are always peddlers selling their own brands of cigarettes. Each one says that his is the one and only one, the best cigarette, and Krishnamurti comes around and says that his is nicotine-free. So the problem is not the gurus, but you. If you don't want to smoke, all these brands will disappear. These gurus are the worst egotists the world has ever seen. All gurus are welfare organizations providing petty experiences to their followers. The guru game is a profitable industry. Try and make two million dollars a year any other way. Even JK, who claims he has no possessions, is the president of an eighty-million-dollar empire.

Choiceless awareness is poppycock. Who is the one being choicelessly aware? You must test this for yourself. That Victorian gentleman has gathered about him the spiritual deadwood of a twenty-, thirty-, and forty-year club. What good is that? I lived with him for years, and I can tell you he is a great actor. "Gentlemen, we are taking a journey together." [laughter] But you can never go on that journey with him. Whatever you do, it is always the same. What you experience with him is the clarification of thought. You are that thought. He is a do-gooder who should have given up long ago.

You have to take my word for it. It never comes into my mind that I am different from you. So when you sit here and ask questions: "Why do they ask me these questions?" There are no answers for these questions at all. Nobody in this world can answer these questions. Whatever answers they give are misleading you. You will end up misguided, misled, misspent, after forty years, fifty years. I know many of these people who have followed these great teachers. Many of them, who have been around Krishnamurti for fifty years, sixty years, are coming and asking me, "Have I wasted forty years, listening to that man?" Do I have to answer that question? You have to answer. I don't have to answer that question. You have wasted fifty years, and you are going to waste another fifty years. You can come here. Nothing will happen, nothing will evolve. You will not get anything from me. That is why I am safe. I live my own life. If somebody comes, I say, "Tell me, what can I do? There's nothing much I can do. Thank you. Good-bye."

[The participants in the following conversation visited UG while attending J. Krishnamurti's annual Saanen camp, nearby UG's Swiss home.]

We want to understand this problem of sorrow.

Look here. Not getting what you want is sorrow. It doesn't matter what you want—happiness, good health, enlightenment. It changes, you know. So, not getting what you want is sorrow.

And that makes us neurotic?

The very nature of mind (if there is a mind) is neurotic, because it wants two things at the same time. So every individual is a neurotic individual. As long as you want two things, you are in a state of neurosis. And when you can't get it, you become psychotic, you become wild. Not that you necessarily go and beat somebody, but you are destroying yourself, because the violence is there inside of you.

What makes you unhappy is the search for a thing that does not exist. Happiness does not exist at all. Similarly, there is no such thing as enlightenment. You may say that every teacher and all the saints and saviors of mankind have been asserting for centuries upon centuries that there is enlightenment and that they are enlightened. Throw them all in one bunch into the river! I don't care. To realize that there is no enlightenment at all is enlightenment. [laughter]

Thought doesn't stop. Thoughts will always be there, because thought and life are not two different things. Don't imagine that you will be free of thoughts. Thoughts may be there or not, but you don't identify yourself with the thoughts at all. There is nothing here to identify itself with a particular movement of thought. They may be there or they may not be there. They are going to be there because life and thought are not two different things. You cannot do a thing about it. When you see that this instrument is not the thing to use to understand anything, then it somehow slows down and falls into its natural rhythm. Then it does not become a problem or a burden to you.

You are trying to understand the teaching of somebody through this instrument, which is a product of this thinking. You do not, while you are listening to somebody, understand that you are using a wrong instrument. Through this, you cannot understand what somebody is saying. That is the first thing you must understand. Whatever you are doing is a barrier to whatever you want to get, it doesn't matter what you want to get. You see, whatever you are doing is adding fuel, adding momentum to that. So, how is that going to slow down or stop, and when are you going to do that? Tomorrow or the day after? You say, "Tomorrow I will understand." There is no tomorrow. This is not going to happen tomorrow. It must happen now or never. So, "I am determined to see what prevents me from understanding what I want to understand." What prevents you from understanding what you want to understand is this very thing that you are using to understand things. This is not my teaching or anybody's teaching, but this is the only thing. You are trying to understand something through an instrument that is not the instrument to understand.

So, the only thing that keeps you trying is the hope, "If I discuss this matter with this chap tomorrow, probably I'll be able to understand." But that is not the way. If I don't understand, I don't understand. "I don't know, I don't seem to have any way of resolving this problem." They have given the example of a dog chasing its own tail. It goes on and on and on, and you feel you are getting somewhere. This is the unfortunate situation. You are not getting anywhere; that is not the way at all. Then what is the way? There is no way. Anything I say, you turn into a way and add to the momentum. That is not the way, that is not the path, it has to be yours. So all paths must go. As long as you follow somebody else's path, the path is the product of thought, so it is actually not a new path. It's the same old path, and you are playing the same old game in a new way. It is not a new game. It is the same old game that you are playing all the time, but you think you are playing a new game. When you see the absurdity of what you are doing, maybe you'll realize, "What the hell have I been doing for thirty years, forty years, fifty years!"

Do I need twenty years to look at that mountain? I don't need twenty years. I don't know how to look at it. (Somebody is explaining a natural state of his being that is yours, not mine.) What happens when you are in front of the thing that you call a mountain, you don't know. (I am describing that state, what actually happens. That is the action I am talking about.) That acts on you. How that action takes place inside of you, and what happens when it acts on you, is a thing you'll never understand. You have to live through this in order to understand what I'm saying. If you had lived through that, you wouldn't be here and you wouldn't ask all these questions. Either you look at it now, or never. And what keeps you trying is the hope, "Maybe next moment I'll be able to understand." You are trying to focus your eyes on what you are looking at and see something more, with more clarity than you saw yesterday. So, all the tricks you are playing—that if you look more carefully, with total attention, there is more clarity in what you are looking at—all this is only deception, because all you are doing is clarifying your thinking. You are not looking at anything. You can't look at anything that way; it doesn't take time. So, "What am I to do with this?" Somebody says, "Look at a flower," so you look at every line, every petal, the color, the depth and so on and so on. If that is not the way, what is the way, and when are you going to look at it that way? You must come to a point where you say, "I simply can't look at it the way that chap is describing. Really, I don't know. Really, I don't seem to be able to look at it any way other than the way I am looking at it." First you must come to that point. That means that what the other chap says must go. All he's told you about how to look at the flower must go. Then you can deal with the way you are looking at the flower. Then you are stuck with it. You really don't know what to do about this at all. You have to come to a point where you can't do anything at all. "This is an impossible task!" You must first deal with this, rather than with what you want to be.

   "A perception without the perceiver"—it's a concept, so the only thing that you can do is think about it. What does this mean, "a perception without the perceiver"? Or "seeing without the seer"? I do not use those words. I say there is no translator who is translating the sensations. They stay pure and simple sensations. There is not even the knowledge that they are sensations. Seeing, tasting, touching, smelling, hearing—these are all the sensations. These five senses are functioning. What happens when these sensations remain as sensations without the translating, you will never know. You are translating all these sensations. So, how to stop doing it? You are lost if you ask, "How am I going to stop the translation?" You can't stop the translation; you are the product of translation. There may not be any stoppage. If some-body says there is a stoppage, to hell with what he is saying. This chap is either a cuckoo or some far out, freaked out ape. He is talking about things that are not real to me. You don't have the courage. You don't want to accept the reality of yourself. What I am saying is something totally unrelated to the way you are functioning. Tomorrow, you say, you want to look at things the way I say I'm looking at them. Maybe I'm deceiving myself. So, "This is the way I'm looking at it. This seems to be the only thing I know. I do not know the perceptions of that chap." So leave that chap alone. It's no use blaming that man or anybody. Nor is there any point in blaming yourself. What is the good of blaming yourself? This is the way you are functioning. So then nat-urally it has to stop. Not stop; it has to slow down. You don't know. You come to a point where you don't know what to do about the whole business. "I can't do anything. This is the only way I know; I don't know any other way. What the other chap says makes no sense to me." So, he says, "Give it a try," and you give it a try, but you don't seem to get anywhere. So, the hope keeps you going. "Tomorrow maybe I'll be able to understand what that chap says. Maybe I'll succeed in doing what he wants me to do." But you will spend the rest of your life try-ing to understand. But if you see the futility of it all, maybe it will stop—not really stop, but slow down.

I can use various similes—the flower, for example. The nature of this human consciousness is to express itself in words; this is its fragrance. Since there are only a handful of people who, not because of what they have or haven't done, have stumbled into this kind of thing, they talk. And when they talk there is bound to be a difference because the man's background is influencing him. You sit and compare this phrase, that phrase, this phrase, that phrase, and then you say that comparatively he says the same thing or he does not. How do you know what that chap is talking about? This is the question I ask, you see. First of all, you do not know what he is talking about. You don't know. You see, if you knew that, you wouldn't come back year after year after year. He may say he talks for the joy of living. I don't know; you'll have to ask him. He knows that you haven't gotten anywhere, and (to be very blunt) you are not going to make it anyhow [laughter], whatever you want. That is a blunt fact. You are not going to make it anyhow, because there is nothing to make, nothing to achieve. This is what I have been trying to communicate to those of you who come to see me and who care to listen to me. As long as you want to get or achieve something or want to be an enlightened man, you are not going to be an enlightened man. Enlightenment is to drop this whole business of wanting to be an enlightened man. That is enlightenment. I don't want to use this word.

So there is enlightenment!

If you want to call it that, you see. I don't know. I never say to myself, "I am an enlightened man, a self-realized man." What does it mean? It doesn't mean anything to me. So to me there's no point in talking about enlightenment, or going about with my head raised, saying to myself and others, "Come ye and listen to me. I am an enlightened man. I am going to liberate you all." That's the holy business. Never. Maybe you are all here from curiosity. Maybe you've heard that there is some funny fellow who is saying the same thing or not the same thing, that he's brutal, he's violent and is blasting that man and saying all sorts of things. Probably curiosity brought you here, I don't know. It is all right with me if you are here from curiosity. And if you say I do all this for kicks, it is all right with me. But I'm not doing it for the kicks. What do I get? All right, assuming for a moment that I am doing all this for pleasure, why do you allow yourself to be used by me? Keep away! Don't allow yourself to be used by me! Stay away! My interest is to send you all packing. Don't allow yourself to be exploited by me! I don't get any pleasure. If you don't come tomorrow, it's all the same. But you don't believe it, because the only thing you know is pleasure. I'm not saying there is anything wrong with pleasure. Don't say that it is something wrong. If you accept that you are here for exactly the same reason that a man goes to a bordello, that's going to give you a terrible shock. There's no difference at all. The people go there every morning, day after day, Sunday after Sunday, at nine o'clock, rushing into the tent [in which J.K. gives his Saanen lectures] for exactly the same reasons. [laughs] You may put it in any refined language that you like. You may say that I am becoming bad more and more.

All this is gibberish talk! I said this to myself in the tent and walked out of it. I said I would never again go to hear him or listen to anybody in this world, not only that man. So then it's finished for you. "What am I here for? What am I listening for?" Perhaps you have heard something about mutation or a transformed individual and that is what is bringing you here. That is what is haunting you; it doesn't let you go to sleep at all. So, that is the real barrier. "I do not want to be haunted by thoughts of sex. I do want to be haunted by thoughts of self-realization, God-realization, enlightenment." You may say they are a far superior thing, but they are exactly the same.

One thing I must say. This is not born out of thinking. This is not a logically ascertained premise that I am putting forth. These are just words springing up from their natural source without any thought, without any thought structure. So take it or leave it! You will be better off if you leave it.

This is the same negative approach that J. Krishnamurti uses.

The problem is that what you call a negative approach is a positive approach. You just call it a negative approach, but you have turned the whole thing into a positive approach. If it is a negative approach, it has to negate itself somewhere along the line. It is very essential to use the negative approach, but you have unfortunately turned the whole negative approach into a positive approach. That man is not responsible for that. Anything this structure touches, it must turn into a positive thing, because it is a product of positive thinking. So anything you listen to is turned into a method, a system. You want to get something through this. For example, somebody says there is a mind and you must uncondition your mind. How are you going to uncondition your mind? You are conditioning your mind through this lingo. That is all that it is necessary for you to see. Don't blame the other chap. I'll sing this song the rest of my life until I drop dead. Whether anybody listens to it or not is of no importance to me. So then you leave this chap alone. You never establish any relationship with this man. The moment you use this to get whatever you want to get, or to arrive at some kind of a destination, you are tricking yourself into the same old game. This you have to see. Seeing is the end. Finished, you see. But you haven't understood a thing; you go there again and again. And you have only clarified your thoughts, and through this so-called clarification you have given strength to the continuity of thought. This is all that has happened. So, it is the hope that keeps you going. You have gotten into a habit, a routine. Instead of going to church, you go there. That's all you are doing.

If you see the absurdity of what you are doing, then there is a possibility of your saying to yourself, "What the hell am I doing? What am I doing? How am I different? Why am I listening to this?"

You appear to oppose spiritual discourses.

I was telling my friends yesterday about a simile we have in one of our books, that those who go to listen to spiritual discourses, those who read books of a religious nature and those who are looking beyond for something are like the monkeys who sit around red ocher, trying to warm themselves. You know what red ocher is. It's red in color, but there's no warmth. There isn't anything you can get from any spiritual discourses or from any religious book. This is what I have been trying to point out to those who care to listen to me. There is nothing to accomplish, nothing to attain. So what's this hullabaloo about? What is it that you want? What is it that you are searching for? This is my question. If you are searching for anything, and you want anything, the first thing you must do is throw away, lock, stock, and barrel, hook, line and sinker, all this stuff that you are hanging on to. You must knock the whole lot into the cocked hat, otherwise there is no chance for you to be yourself.

If you follow any path, it doesn't matter what that path is, it is always leading you astray. It is putting you on the wrong path. If you make anything out of what I am saying you are lost, body and soul, and if there is a God, he must, out of his sheer mercy, save you all and save you from me.

One thing I make very clear. I'm not here to liberate you at all. Who am I to liberate you? What is it that you want to liberate yourself from? You are trying to ask for a thing that you have. So I only point out that you're on the wrong track, and you're asking me, "What is the right track? What am I to do?" Are you ready to accept the fact that you are on the wrong track? That means that the teacher you are running after and the stuff you are thinking about—that's the very thing that must go. Are you ready to throw it out of the window? Hm? You have a hope that one day that's going to lead you where you want to get to. That's the problem, you know.

Your teacher must go, it doesn't matter who the teacher is. The very thing that you are reading—that's the very thing you must be free from. Many of you will be hurt if I point out to you this thing. There's a book you'll find there on the shelf, *Freedom from the Known* [by JK]. It's a very fancy title. So, you are reading that book. That's the very thing you must be free from in order to be free. What you are reading there, you must be free from. If that gentleman has failed to free himself and to free you from what you are reading there, he has failed. You may not be willing to blame him; you are ready to blame yourself. That's the unfortunate situation you find yourself in today. It's your problem, not his. Leave him alone.

What do we have when we've dropped this searching?

You want to be assured beforehand. You see, a path means that you are trying to arrive at a destination. The word *path* is a mystical word. What is the path you are following? Somebody is telling you, "This is the way. You must free yourself from the conditioning. That is the path," for example. But it is always misleading you. It is not leading you anywhere. You are moving away from yourself. You have to be yourself, and his path is trying to turn you into something other than yourself. Why do you want to be somebody other than yourself? You see, otherwise you wouldn't listen to anyone.

Look here. You want to be full of feeling for everybody. Somebody is talking about love, for example, so you want to be full of that love, whatever it is. You don't know a damned thing about what that chap or anybody else is talking about. So, you want to be full of that. You are projecting a hundredfold what you think love is, for example. So that's what makes it difficult for you to be yourself. And that you are going to be only tomorrow or the day after.

It's not a path; we're making a path out of it.

So, if you don't want to go anywhere, where is the need for you to look for a path?

Sentient Publications, LLC publishes books on cultural creativity, experimental education, transformative spirituality, holistic health, new science, and ecology, approached from an integral viewpoint. Our authors are intensely interested in exploring the nature of life from fresh perspectives, addressing life's great questions, and fostering the full expression of the human potential. Sentient Publication's books arise from the spirit of inquiry and the richness of the inherent dialogue between writer and reader.

We are very interested in hearing from our readers. To direct suggestions or comments to us, or to be added to our mailing list, please contact:

SENTIENT PUBLICATIONS, LLC

1113 Spruce Street
Boulder, CO 80302
303.443.2188
contact@sentientpublications.com
www.sentientpublications.com